# Student Assessment

## *Fast, Frequent, Formative*

### Debra J. Dirksen

ROWMAN & LITTLEFIELD EDUCATION
A division of
ROWMAN & LITTLEFIELD
Lanham • Boulder • New York • Toronto • Plymouth, UK

Published by Rowman & Littlefield Education
A division of Rowman & Littlefield
4501 Forbes Boulevard, Suite 200, Lanham, Maryland 20706
www.rowman.com

10 Thornbury Road, Plymouth PL6 7PP, United Kingdom

British Library Cataloguing in Publication Information Available

**Library of Congress Cataloging-in-Publication Data**

Dirksen, Debra J. (Debra Jean)
Student assessment : fast, frequent, and formative / Debra Dirksen.
pages cm.
Includes bibliographical references and index.
ISBN 978-1-4758-0120-0 (pbk. : alk. paper) -- ISBN 978-1-4758-0121-7 (electronic)
1. Educational tests and measurements--United States. I. Title.
LB3051.D568 2013
371.260973--dc23
2013029043

♾™ The paper used in this publication meets the minimum requirements of American National Standard for Information Sciences Permanence of Paper for Printed Library Materials, ANSI/NISO Z39.48-1992.

Printed in the United States of America

# Contents

# Preface

One of our greatest concerns as teachers is helping students master the content. Unfortunately, many times students do not come to our classrooms with the prerequisite skills needed to master that content. When I was a middle school math teacher, my primary concern was that my students gain the skills they needed in order to be successful in the world of mathematics. I wanted them to master the content, but many times they lacked the foundational skills needed to be successful. When teaching eighth-grade math, I was amazed at the number of students who entered my classroom without basic arithmetic skills.

One year I had a student who did not have the slightest idea of how to do long division. He could make the problem look right, but the numbers made absolutely no sense. He had made it almost all the way to high school without a teacher's realizing that he didn't know how to do long division. He presented himself as a competent, confident student, and somehow no one ever looked beyond the facade to see a student who needed to stop and learn a foundational skill that was key to his success in mathematics. By implementing formative assessment in my classroom, I was able to help this student and other students as well. Using the metaphor so aptly applied in video gaming, I allow students to "press the reset button" to stop instruction, take a step back, and learn the concepts they need to master.

I wrote this book for this student and students like him. Too often, students are passed from one grade to another, from one course to another, even though they haven't gained the foundational skills they need to be successful in the next grade or course. We could stop and fail all students who don't master the content. We could give up on those students who don't master the content and let them move on to become the next teacher's problem. Or we could stop and take the time to teach students while they are still in our classroom. I believe that it is my job as a teacher to make sure my students are learning the content being taught. I try to never assume that just because I'm teaching, my students are learning. I use formative assessment as an essential part of my own teaching to become aware of those students who are not mastering the content. If I can make sure that all students leave my classroom with the foundational skills they will need in order to be successful as they continue their educational careers, I feel that I have been successful as their teacher.

I open this book by looking more closely at the concept of using formative assessment as a tool for students to "press the reset button." So many times we are so focused on covering the material that we don't take the time to make sure our students are learning what we are teaching. In today's schools, we require that time be held constant and learning be allowed to vary. In order to progress with the content, it seems okay that some students will learn everything while other students will learn less than they need to learn. Formative assessment gives us a tool to let time vary, rather than letting learning vary. It allows us to stop and make sure our students are mastering key skills and concepts. Some students need more time to master the material, and applying the concept of pressing the reset button allows them the extra time they need. Through the use of formative assessment, we can ensure that students do indeed master those skills and concepts.

In this book, I provide both an overview of formative assessment, its purpose, and tools for record keeping, analysis, and implementation, and also detailed information on specific assessment strategies that can be used as formative assessment tools in the classroom. My goal is that every reader find multiple strategies that they can take and use to implement formative assessment in their own classroom. I want to give teachers specific tools they can use to support student learning. I want teachers to be able to take the time to focus on learning, allowing their students to "press the reset button" through the use of formative assessment until they master the concept being taught.

I hope this book becomes a valuable part of your personal library.

# ONE

## "Press the Reset Button"

Why are video games so engaging and motivating? One reason may be that in a video game, if a player starts a game at level 1 or 2 and things start going wrong, and they realize they don't have many of the capabilities they should have gained to be successful, they press the reset button and begin again. In video games, failure is good. Players start the game over so they can learn and gain the skills necessary to move on through this level and to the next.

The gaming industry has learned what we educators need to learn: the ability to press reset is motivating. The players use this as a tool to learn and gain the skills necessary to be successful at the game (Morgan 2008). How can we build into instruction the idea that failure is an integral part of learning? How can we facilitate learning through failure rather than learning to fear failure? We can do this by putting in place tools that allow students to press that virtual reset button.

### TIME AND LEARNING

As teachers, we can give students a means for pressing the reset button by making use of formative assessments. Formative assessments are typically ongoing evaluations that are completed to inform instructional decisions. When used appropriately, they provide us with a tool to guide the design and implementation of learning activities and lessons.

Too many times we teach a unit, give a test, look at the results, and move on to the next unit regardless of the outcome. Sometimes it feels as though the only measures of student learning we find of value are those tests we utilize to assign a grade in a course. We need to get beyond summative evaluations and examine the possibilities of using formative assessments to enable us to better meet the needs of our students.

1

In education, we've made the decision to hold time constant and let learning vary. Classes occur over a specified amount of time, and it is presumed that students will learn the material within that given time frame. In reality, we learn at different rates; some need more time, some less. Additionally, students don't all learn in the same way. We are different, and sometimes the way we think and teach doesn't work for our students and how they think and learn. We need to design instruction in a manner that will let time vary and hold learning constant. To help students be successful, we need to provide them with a reset button to press. The reset button is formative assessment.

In reality (at least, in the reality of formal education), time has to be held constant. It's difficult to give students varying amounts of time to learn the material, given the structure of the semester system. Within that limit, however, we can allow time to vary to a degree. We can take the time to realize when our students don't understand. We can take the time to identify those key basic skills and competencies they need in order to be successful in our class and to move on to the next level. We can take the time to teach those skills.

We have taught our children to fear failure. Teachers, parents, and administrators do everything they can to ensure that students never experience failure, interceding whenever possible to ensure that the child succeeds. Failure is portrayed as being bad. This has a negative impact on student achievement. Learning occurs best when delivered at an optimal level of challenge, which puts the student in the direct line of failure. To help students work and learn "on the edge" and reach an optimal level of challenge, the teacher needs to take advantage of formative assessment, using it as a tool to teach students how to learn from failure rather than to fear failure. We need to allow students to press the reset button through their own use of formative assessment.

## LEARNED FEAR

When we were young we knew no fear. If you ask a four-year-old if he or she can do something, nine times out of ten the answer will be yes, no matter what we ask. Ask a child "Can you learn to read?" "Can you run as fast as the wind?" "Can you climb this tree?"—and the answer will likely be yes. As they grow older, children begin to learn fear. On the playground they are slow to learn fear, but in the classroom fear comes easily.

We teach students to fear failure. It's not okay to fail, especially academically. If they don't learn a new concept or skill, we feel that they just aren't trying hard enough. In many schools, students are labeled and grouped and placed into settings where everyone knows which groups the smart kids are in and which groups the slow learners are in. The slow learners are the ones in the bluebird group or the ones in Mrs. Jones's class. We group students homogenously, so the teacher can more easily meet the needs of the students.

To achieve this we track students, classes, and, many times, entire schools. We have the smart kids' class, the middle-of-the-road class, and the class where the kids who just aren't getting it are sent to be remediated, along with thirty or forty other kids. Consideration has also been given to passing laws that require schools to retain students who fail to perform key standards at grade level, putting an end to social promotion. If students are unable to perform at grade level they are labeled in one fashion or another. While opportunities for remediation may have been provided, many times it is too little too late. The message is conveyed: failure is bad.

## FEAR OF FAILURE AND ITS IMPACT ON STUDENT LEARNING

Given scenarios as described in the previous section, when a child reaches school age he or she begins to fear failure. An adult's negative response when a student fails to complete a learning activity or demonstrate a specific skill communicates to the student that failure is bad. Students who have a fear of failure may be reluctant to venture into the unfamiliar and face new challenges. They are only willing to complete those tasks or learn skills at which they know they will be successful. They may almost seem to sabotage themselves and their ability to succeed at a new task.

Students who fear failure may procrastinate completing a task, making success less likely. Though they may have set goals for themselves, students may not follow through on tasks that would allow them to reach those goals. Their anxiety may be so high that they may not even try to complete a task or reach for a goal. Frequently students who fear failure have low self-esteem or self-confidence, often thinking that they are not good enough or smart enough to achieve academically.

Attitudes such as these have a negative impact on student learning. Students who come to school fearing failure, especially those who not only fear failure but also have limited confidence in their own ability to learn, are not as likely to be successful in the classroom. Some students become so stymied by fear of failure that they choose not to try. "If I try and don't succeed I will be labeled dumb. If I don't try at all, I don't succeed because I choose not to try." Fear of failure also contributes to test anxiety, so that students may not perform as well on high-stakes assessments or summative assessments. To reduce the negative effects that come with fearing failure, we need to teach students the value of failure and how it can help us learn and reach higher levels within a discipline.

## THE VALUE OF FAILURE

Failure is a wonderful learning tool. We learn the most from our mistakes. We need to learn to think of failure as a means to learning. Inventors, entrepreneurs, and designers make a lot of mistakes as they work to discover and to build new ideas (Brown, Kiefer, and Schlesinger 2012). If failure is internalized it becomes disempowering for the individual. To bring value, each student needs to unlearn those habits associated with the negative perceptions of failure. "As Col. Casey Haskins, who heads up military instruction for West Point, has said, 'You have to make it cool to fail'" (Sims 2012).

Failure provides us with the opportunity to look at a problem with clarity. It gives us the opportunity to step back and examine a situation and figure out why we were wrong. We are able to analyze our efforts and the problem at hand and use it as a tool to enhance learning, building connections between our prior knowledge and the concepts we are currently learning. What we learn from our mistakes is most easily remembered and transferred to new situations.

So failure not only allows us to better retain new information, but it also gives us a means to develop new understandings and to learn how to learn. It's a metacognitive tool, giving us an opportunity to reflect on our learning experiences and allowing us to learn from our mistakes. This is best achieved when we work within that optimal level of challenge, where we can make mistakes and have the capacity to analyze those mistakes and work toward a new solution.

## OPTIMAL LEVEL OF CHALLENGE

Vygotsky (1978) identified the zone of proximal development as the frame between what a student can do with help and that which the student can do independently. The zone of proximal development is the optimal level of challenge needed to enhance student learning. It is the level that is challenging enough to keep students engaged and interested in the learning activity, but not so challenging that they become frustrated.

If content is too easy and not challenging enough, students will be bored and will not benefit from the learning activity. If content is too difficult, they will be frustrated and unable to learn from their mistakes. The key is designing instruction so that learning activities are at a level that challenges the students and engages them. It needs to be at a level where students can fail, reflect, and with appropriate support from the teacher, learn from their mistakes.

We can use working within the Zone of Proximal Development as a guide to what our students should learn next about a given discipline.

Key to this is an understanding of the students' prior knowledge of the content and related concepts. Working from the students' prior knowledge, we need to determine, given the breadth and depth of any given content, what would be best or easiest for the students to learn next. Essentially we scaffold our students in their development, working from where they are in their current knowledge, skills, and understanding to where they need to be.

We determine the sequencing so that we can create a learning ladder for our students, helping them grow and develop academically, always challenging them but providing the support so that they can be successful. Unfortunately, this learning ladder will not be the same for all students. We need to be prepared to work with our students, to identify the needs of each student and to design scaffolds that will meet their individual needs and start from where they are.

Just because a student has taken the prerequisite course does not mean that he or she will have the prerequisite knowledge to be successful in your class. This is where we need to start teaching our students how to learn. Most importantly, this is where we need to start teaching our students how to learn from their mistakes and how to make failure a learning tool.

## LEARNING FROM FAILURE

To learn from failure, our response to student failure and the students' response to their own failure need to change. Taking a lesson from research conducted on entrepreneurs (Brown, Kiefer, and Schlesinger 2012; Brown 2012), we need to teach our students to first take one small step forward and take an action. For some it will be like taking a step off a cliff and risking falling into a dark abyss. But the first step in learning that failure is our friend is to try something that is outside of our comfort zone.

That first step may be attempting to solve a math problem, write a paragraph, or speak in a foreign language. Second, the learner needs to step back and analyze the outcome of his or her action: How did it go? What did I learn from that action? In solving a math problem, was I able to follow all of the steps? Was there a point of confusion where I wasn't sure of the next step in solving the problem? Do I understand the process and purpose of the mathematics involved in solving the problem? Did I make mistakes along the way? Were the mistakes basic arithmetic issues, or was there a larger concept I didn't understand?

Finally, after they reflect on their work, we need to build what the students learned from their experience into their future work and learning. By following this process, they can learn to analyze their own experiences and mistakes, and to use those failures as tools from which to build their own learning and understanding.

If we have students working in the zone of proximal development, outside of that independent zone where they don't really need our support as a teacher, we need to be prepared to scaffold or mediate our students' learning. Scaffolding involves not only clearly defining the task for the students, but it also requires the teacher to provide direct instruction and support materials that walk the student, step by step, through a learning activity or process such as problem solving (using the scientific method) or writing a five-paragraph essay.

For example, when teaching her students how to solve word problems, a colleague provided three levels of support for her students. Students who were already skilled in identifying relevant information in a word problem and selecting the proper equations to use were asked to move forward and work with more difficult problems. Students who just needed a little guidance were provided with a few examples and some guided practice. But students who really did not understand how to determine relevant information or select a formula were provided additional support.

The teacher created a guide that walked the students through a series of problems. Initially, each guide was specific to the problem. Then as students developed skill, a more general outline for solving word problems was provided. She differentiated the lesson so that advanced students could move ahead, and middle-level students were provided support so that they could move forward independently. By doing so she was able to focus her attention on the students who really did not understand the process. She specified each step and sequenced the activity for the students who needed that level of support.

Scaffolding may include helping the students with planning, organizing, doing, or reflecting on the task that was assigned. The level of scaffolding should match the needs of the student. For some students you will need to define the process with clear, specific, written directions. Other students may need only a brief outline, and others may need to be allowed to explore independently, with limited direction.

Wood, Bruner, and Ross (1976) described six functions the teacher should fulfill as he or she works to scaffold students' instruction:

1. Orient the students' attention to the task.
2. Reduce the number of steps required to solve a problem, simplifying the problem so that the individual learner can handle the components of the process.
3. Maintain the students' involvement with the activity, motivating the students and directing their actions as necessary.
4. Highlight critical features of the task for the students.
5. Control the frustration of the students and the risk of failure.

6. Provide the students with examples of the actions required in completing the activity.

Scaffolding provides the teacher a means for helping students venture outside of their comfort zone and undertake tasks that are more difficult. This in effect expands their individual zone of proximal development. As we provide support, allowing students to complete more difficult tasks successfully, they will be able to grow more rapidly. As students grow in their confidence and capabilities, they will be able to grasp even more difficult concepts and skills. And as we teach them to step back and reflect on their actions and learn from their mistakes, their confidence, retention, and abilities will likewise grow and develop.

## STOP AND LEARN

Just like when they play video games, students must be allowed to press the reset button, take a step back, and master the skills they have not yet mastered. Of greatest importance are the foundational skills that are required for students to be successful in learning more complex concepts. Within a discipline, we should work with our students to apply to the classroom what they know so well from playing video games. Making mistakes is okay, and failure can play a big part in the learning process.

To take advantage of the "reset button," we need to redefine failure in our classrooms. We can teach our students that if they learned something from the experience, then they did not fail. If our students know that success occurs when they gain experience and skills and move toward their goals, then they will be more motivated to learn new things. In reality, failure only occurs when we refuse to try. We don't have to be the best at something to be a success.

We can teach our students that they just need to try their best, and possibly to try again, and they will be a success. Our classrooms should become places where we celebrate trying. Each time we fail we have the opportunity to learn something. We can apply what we have learned toward what we want to achieve. As the teacher, we can share how our own "failures" provided us with opportunities to learn. We can tell our students about how we overcame failure and what we learned from that experience. We can manage our classrooms in such a way as to allow the students to feel comfortable with pressing the reset button in the academic world.

## CONCLUSION

As we look at teaching our students that failure is a tool that supports learning and as we design a classroom climate that views success as trying our hardest to meet new challenges, we need to look for assessment tools that will give us the feedback we can use to foster learning. This is where formative assessment comes in. It will serve as the "reset button" in the classroom. It will provide teacher and student the feedback needed to track learning. It will also help the teacher determine the best learning route for the students.

In the following chapters we will explore the use of formative assessment as a learning tool. The next two chapters will discuss the purpose of formative assessment and how to design formative assessments that are valid and reliable. The remainder of the text will be dedicated to specific examples of formative assessments that can be utilized to inform instruction. These serve as a "reset button" for students, letting the teacher know when and where they need assistance in learning the content.

The chapters are aligned with the learning process, beginning at the beginning with preassessments that can be utilized to determine where students currently are in relation to the content being taught and then moving on through formative assessments that can be easily implemented as part of the teaching process. Each chapter will provide examples of how each assessment is implemented, and the data collection procedures are outlined. Procedures are outlined to help teachers easily gather and implement the data gained so that it can be efficiently used to impact teaching and learning.

# TWO

# Formative Assessment: Purpose

As teachers, we can give the student a way to "press the reset button" by using formative assessments. Formative assessments are typically ongoing evaluations that inform teaching decisions. When used appropriately, they provide us with a tool to guide the design and implementation of learning activities and lessons.

In this chapter we will discuss the purpose of the formative assessment process and its implementation in the classroom to promote learning for all students. We will explore the purpose of formative assessment and how we can use formative assessment to inform instruction. We will discuss the use of formative assessment and the role it plays in the response to intervention (RTI) process. We will also discuss how formative assessment can be used in the design of instruction, using performance data to guide the design of instruction so that we can provide students with the time they need to learn the foundational skills in order to be successful. Finally, we will explore the application of backward design principles and formative assessment data as we strive to meet students' learning needs.

## FORMATIVE ASSESSMENT

Formative assessment has a definite purpose in the classroom. Primarily, formative assessment serves to inform instruction and thereby support student learning. Robert Stake said it best: "When the cook tastes the soup, that's formative: when the guests taste the soup, that's summative" (Scriven 1991, 169). As the cook, the teacher needs to stop and taste the soup before moving forward with instruction. By using formative assessments, we can ensure that our students understand and master the key basic skills and competencies they need to be successful in our classroom.

Formative assessments should be conducted in a manner that will allow us, as teachers, to use the information to improve instructional methods and learning strategies.

Formative assessment begins while planning instruction. It is a process of identifying the learning outcomes to be associated with the unit being designed and prioritizing the learning goals associated with individual lessons. We need to determine those goals that are key to student learning and their continued success with the content as it increases in difficulty and complexity. After identifying these key learning outcomes, we can then identify ways to formatively assess the students' progress in meeting these objectives. By formatively assessing student growth on specific outcomes, we can review the data with an eye toward giving constructive feedback to students that is designed to improve their performance, in addition to using the data to inform continued instruction.

Formative assessments range from the simplistic to the surreal. The easiest are sometimes the best. Simple observation is a handy tool for formative assessments. Looking for those confused expressions and watching closely as students work on guided practice allows us to identify students who don't understand a concept. During presentations and lectures, we can ask lots of questions. Engaging students in discussion during a directed presentation allows you to know if they understand the material. It also allows you to redesign instruction on the spot or use another tactic during your presentation, such as providing a specific example, metaphor, or varied explanations. The most effective use of formative assessment is when it is used daily, as an integral part of the instructional process, supporting teaching and learning on a minute-by-minute basis (Foster and Poppers 2009).

To be an effective learning tool, formative assessment requires a learning environment that is collaborative, nonjudgmental, and built upon the belief that the students and teachers compose a team. The feedback provided by formative assessments needs to be used by both the teacher and the students.

While we need to track students' progress, the students also need to be engaged in tracking their own progress. Data books, in which students record their own learning progress, and specific written feedback from the teacher can be used by the students to guide their work and reinforce their efforts and learning accomplishments (Marzano 2007).

Data books are like the score cards kept by athletes as they track their own performance, similar to baseball players' score cards as they track their batting average, home runs, strike-outs, runs batted in (RBIs), and on-base percentage. Formative assessment becomes the "reset button" allowing the students and the teacher to recognize when it is time to stop, reflect, and perhaps reteach concepts that, if not fully understood, will interfere with the students' ultimate learning success.

## INFORMING INSTRUCTION

One of the key purposes of formative assessment is to inform instruction. It is a cyclical process that may be completed once or multiple times during each lesson or unit. The formative assessment process involves more than just giving and grading a test. It also requires the teacher to review the results of the assessment, looking at student work and identifying common approaches, errors, and misconceptions.

After the data is gathered and analyzed, we need to reflect on the results and not only consider the pedagogical approach we utilized during our initial instruction but also reflect on our own knowledge of the content we just assessed. We may need to expand our own knowledge of the content as well as consider other instructional strategies to use in reteaching concepts. After collecting and analyzing student work, reflecting on their responses, and considering content that needs to be retaught, we need to design lessons to reengage the students with the content and then teach the new lesson (Foster and Poppers 2009).

As we utilize formative assessment to inform instruction, we need to remember to not just reteach the same lesson. We need to get the students to think about the concepts differently. When reteaching, the new lessons need to be tied back directly to the results of the formative assessment (Foster and Poppers 2009). Utilize your findings regarding common errors and misconceptions to design whole group instruction.

Also differentiate instruction for students who need extra help in learning the content, as well as for those who have already mastered the skills. Of key importance is solidifying foundational concepts that students must know in order to be successful with other related content as they progress within the discipline. Without the foundational knowledge, students will be unsuccessful as the content becomes more difficult.

## RESPONSE TO INTERVENTION

Formative assessment is an integral part of the response to intervention (RTI) process. The role of RTI is to address the needs of students who are not succeeding in the general education classroom. It is a tool designed to address the needs of these students by helping teachers implement research-based interventions (National Dissemination Center for Children with Disabilities [NICHCY] 2012). The intent is to help all students achieve academically.

RTI is a multilevel prevention system that incorporates progress monitoring, data-informed decision making, and a screening process to implement instructional strategies that are culturally relevant and have demonstrated the capability to improve student learning outcomes. Formative assessments play a key role in RTI as a tool to monitor student progress. Assessment data, including formative assessment data, is used to determine when students have not learned core learning objectives and are at risk of performing below their level of capability.

Instructional interventions can be implemented to help students master these key concepts. Depending on the students' responsiveness, the nature and intensity of the intervention is modified. If the learning issue cannot be resolved instructionally, findings are utilized to identify students with learning disabilities or other disabilities.

As detailed by NICHCY (2012), in Tier 1 of the RTI process students who have failed to learn instructional objectives are retaught key concepts using an instructional strategy designed to be used with small groups or possibly with the whole class. Each student's progress is tracked closely. If students respond to the instruction, the learning issue is determined to be related to insufficient instruction, and modifications continue. The focus is on assisting all students to be successful. The use of formative assessment to track student progress and identify learning issues continues, whether Tier 1 interventions were successful or not.

If a student is not responsive to the instructional strategy within a reasonable time frame (not more than six to eight weeks), Tier 2 is implemented. In Tier 2 the intensity of the instructional intervention implemented is greater and more closely targeted to the specific areas in which the student is having difficulty. Again, the student's progress is closely monitored with formative assessments.

For example, a student may not have mastered a basic arithmetic skill such as multiplication. Without this foundational knowledge, students will have difficulty with long division, determining the least common denominator, and other math skills that build upon basic multiplication. Again, if the student shows appropriate progress, instruction will continue with the student's learning needs met. For many students, if learning issues are identified early and addressed with effective instruction, the student will be able to progress without further issues.

If a student is still unable to learn the required core concepts with Tier 2 interventions, a third level is implemented with yet more intensive interventions. Instruction at this level is typically individualized. If students do not respond to Tier 3 interventions, then they are referred for full evaluation to possibly receive special education services. The data accumulated via formative assessments implemented at Tiers 1, 2, and 3 become part of the documentation reviewed in determining the student's need for special services outside of the regular classroom.

As described above, formative assessment is essential to the RTI process in monitoring student progress and to inform instructional decisions. Progress monitoring involves the constant review of student progress, checking for understanding of key concepts and skills. As with all formative assessments, the intent is to identify where individual students are not learning those learning objectives.

As described earlier in the chapter, the monitoring of student progress is integral to the teaching and learning process, and data on student achievement should be gathered at multiple points during instruction. The data gathered is used to inform instructional decisions to modify instruction to meet individual student learning needs and to differentiate instruction based on those needs.

## HOLDING LEARNING CONSTANT AND LETTING TIME VARY

In formal education, we've made the decision to hold time constant and let learning vary. Classes occur over a specified amount of time, and it is presumed that students will learn the material within that given time frame. In reality, we learn at different rates: some students need more time, some less. In addition, all students don't learn in the same way. Sometimes the way we think and teach doesn't work for how our students think and learn. Ideally, we should design instruction in a manner that will let time vary and hold learning constant.

However, this is difficult in reality because time has to be held constant. It is difficult to give students varying amounts of time to learn the material within the structure of the school year. But within the limits imposed on us, we can allow for some variation. We can take the time to check the students' comprehension. We can take the time to identify the key basic skills and competencies that they must master in order to be successful in our class and move on to the next level, and we can take the time to teach students those skills.

Formative assessment provides us the tool we need in order to hold learning constant, especially when teaching students the core concepts necessary to being successful as they progress in the discipline. By monitoring students' progress, we can accelerate learning by providing instruction that aligns with their specific learning needs. When students have the foundational knowledge and skills necessary to be successful, they will be able to progress at a faster rate.

Consider the following example: Peter had missed an extended period of school at a critical time in elementary school and was placed in a learning disabled classroom. The staff believed that he had a learning disability, when in reality Peter had missed a key mathematics concept, multiplication. After being remediated by a special education teacher, Peter was mainstreamed into the eighth-grade math class. The teacher preassessed students, and not knowing that Peter had just left the learning disabled classroom, she placed him in her highest group. Peter went on to receive an A in the class.

For Peter, remediation worked. He was able to progress at a faster rate, learning the content he had failed to learn because he did not understand multiplication. While this intervention took years, if applied on a regular basis formative assessment can help hold learning constant and let time vary, allowing students to learn in a manner and at a pace that best meets their learning needs.

## DESIGNING INSTRUCTION WITH THE END IN MIND

"To begin with the end in mind means to start with a clear understanding of your destination. It means to know where you're going so that you better understand where you are now so that the steps you take are always in the right direction" (Covey 1994, 98). This quote describes the intent of a unit planning model known as backward design.

The backward design model includes three stages, each beginning with the end in mind: (1) identify desired results, (2) determine acceptable evidence, and (3) plan learning experiences and instruction. The backward design model works well when developing differentiated instruction. When differentiating instruction, lessons are designed to meet the needs of students as identified through formative assessment.

With backward design the instructional strategies and learning activities are not identified until after first determining the learning goals and objectives and how each will be assessed. In the first stage, the overall needs of the students, based upon preassessment data and the learning outcomes identified from content standards, are utilized to identify the desired outcomes.

Learning outcomes are prioritized and grounded in the content to be taught. They range from those objectives that all students should know and be able to do to those objectives that are worth knowing but are not a priority for all learners. Overarching these key concepts are the big ideas and deep understandings that we want all students to learn from the unit, regardless of their learning abilities.

In the second stage the learning outcomes to be taught in the unit are aligned with assessments that will provide evidence of the students' achievement. At this point, summative as well as formative assessments are identified. We need to consider what assessments will best let us know that the students have achieved the objectives and met our expectations. Also, we need to consider the evidence that would allow us to assess in-depth understanding as opposed to a superficial understanding. As we identify formative assessments, we need to consider evidence that best helps us guide our instruction.

Backward design helps us think in terms of how we will assess student performance. Assessment, especially formative assessment, is the crux of backward design. The focus is on ensuring that the students learn the identified concepts and skills rather than on covering the content. Formative assessment is also integral to the final stage of backward design, in which instructional strategies and learning opportunities are planned and designed.

Learning activities should be designed to engage the students as well as to promote in-depth understanding. Strategies should be clearly aligned with the outcomes they are designed to teach, as well as with the assessments that will be utilized to evaluate student learning. These same learning activities can also be used to formatively assess learning of the outcomes.

As described with backward design, formative assessment begins while planning instruction. By so doing we can make sure that students have a clear understanding of the content and the foundational skills they will need to be successful learners. If we merely cover the content, they may leave our classroom with misunderstandings and without the knowledge that will help them progress in the discipline. Formative assessment is a key tool we can use as we design, develop, and implement instruction, with the goal of ensuring that all of our students will have the opportunity to learn in our classroom.

## MEETING STUDENT LEARNING NEEDS

As stated above, in terms of RTI, backward design, and the need to hold learning constant rather than time, the primary purpose of formative assessment is to meet student learning needs. Too often, we teach a unit of instruction, give a test, look at the results, and move on to the next unit regardless of the outcome. Sometimes it feels as though the only measures of student learning we value are the tests we use to assign a grade in a course.

We need to move beyond these summative evaluations and examine the possibilities of using formative assessment to better meet the needs of our students. We need to design instruction so that students can press the reset button and go back to learn what they didn't get the first time.

Formative assessment has been shown to improve student learning across grade levels, pre-K to 20. Formative assessment supports learning for both low-performing and high-performing students (Black and Wiliam 1998a; McCurdy and Shapiro 1992; Fuchs and Fuchs 1986). By providing feedback related to specific errors with suggestions for improvement, we enable students to improve their performance (Vispoel and Austin 1995; Wininger 2005). When students have a clear understanding of the learning objectives and assessment criteria and are given the opportunity to reflect on their performance, student learning also improves (Ross 2006; Ruiz-Primo and Furtak 2006).

## CONCLUSION

Formative assessment serves multiple purposes. First and foremost, it increases the impact of instruction on student learning. If the teacher and the students track student learning, that information can be used to improve performance, just as data on batting average, free throws, and yardage gained is used in athletics to improve the performance of the athlete.

As students track their growth in a content area, they will be motivated to implement learning strategies that will help them continue to grow academically. Formative assessment data also serves to inform instruction, allowing the teacher to alter instruction in a timely manner to address individual learning needs. More formally, formative assessment supports RTI, providing a tool that is used to monitor student progress as interventions are implemented to address individual learning needs.

Finally, formative assessment provides the teacher with a tool that can be used to hold learning constant and let time vary. When we know that a student has not mastered a foundational skill or concept, we can stop and take the time to intervene before the student (and the learning opportunity) is lost. By tracking student learning, we can make sure that each student masters key concepts at an appropriate level before moving forward.

The formative assessment process is an instructional tool that needs to be implemented consistently and regularly. The focus is on meeting individual learning needs from the moment we design a lesson until the final exam is given, making sure that no child is left behind.

# THREE

# Formative Assessment: Reliability and Validity

Reliability and validity are just as important when designing formative assessments as they are with summative or high-stakes assessments. Assessments must be designed to support the interpretations that are made from the data that has been gathered. To do so, the assessments must be reliable and valid. In this chapter we will discuss the implementation of methods for ensuring the validity and reliability of formative assessments.

## DIFFERENCE BETWEEN VALIDITY AND RELIABILITY

Of utmost importance in assessment is the assurance that the instruments that are used align with the objectives that are being evaluated and are accurate and consistent in their results. Evaluating the validity and reliability of our formative assessments provides us with these assurances. When an assessment is deemed valid, it is said to evaluate what it is purported to evaluate. Therefore, there is alignment between the assessment and the content that is being assessed. Reliability, on the other hand, indicates that the measure is consistent. If an assessment is administered one time and then readministered, with no intervening instruction or intervention, the test results will be the same.

Validity has been deemed by some to be the most important characteristic when determining the quality of an assessment. It refers to the degree to which an assessment measures what it claims to measure. In other words, validity is the extent to which the data gathered from the assessment support the interpretations to be made based on those data. "Without validity, an assessment is useless" (Educational Testing Service

[ETS] 2003). An assessment with a high level of validity will be closely linked with the test's intended focus.

When applying this to formative assessments, it means that the items used in the assessment will be closely related to the objectives they are meant to assess. If the objective indicates that the students will be able to compare and contrast two concepts, then the assessment used to evaluate that objective must reflect the students' ability to compare and contrast elements of those concepts. The more direct the alignment between the learning outcome being assessed and the measure, the higher the validity of the assessment will be. With good validity, the teacher will be able to confidently use the data gathered from the assessment to inform his or her instructional decisions and to differentiate instruction based upon the students' individual needs.

Reliability is equally important. One of the best examples of reliability is your bathroom scale. Each time you weigh yourself, the results should be the same if you are not gaining or losing weight. The results should be consistent and reproducible. The same is true of formative assessments. The assessment must provide consistent, reproducible results over time. Within the assessment, items addressing the same learning objective must also be internally consistent, each providing similar results as to the student's comprehension of the objective. In order to make valid inferences about a student's skills and capabilities, based upon the results of an assessment, the instrument used must also be reliable.

The two measures, validity and reliability, are intertwined with formative assessment and the use of data from the assessments to make informed instructional decisions. The assessment must be valid and reliable when using the assessment to support the design of instruction to improve student learning. If a test is inconsistent in the results it provides or does not align with the identified learning objectives, the data has no value, particularly for instructional purposes. An assessment must be valid and reliable, or the results will be misinterpreted, unfair, and may actually hamper a student's learning.

## VALIDITY AND FORMATIVE ASSESSMENT

The purpose of formative assessment is to improve learning. As said previously, the validity of a measure is based on the ability of the assessment to meet the intent of the assessment. Given these parameters, to be valid the formative assessment must improve learning. The threats to validity for formative assessment are things that keep the assessment from providing data that can be used to inform instructional decisions and to improve student learning.

When designing formative assessments, there must be a clear understanding about what you want the students to learn. The assessment must address these objectives with enough breadth and depth so that you can have a clear understanding of the students' ability to master the outcome. There needs to be direct and specific alignment between the objectives and the assessment. When there is not a clear alignment between the assessment and the learning goals, it is called "construct underrepresentation." For example, if a multiple-choice assessment were utilized to determine a student's ability to write a five-paragraph essay, there would be construct underrepresentation.

Another common issue that impacts validity occurs when the assessment is designed in such a manner that it assesses something other than the identified objectives. This is called "construct irrelevant variance." For example, an assessment may align with the objectives but may be written in such a way that it assesses a student's reading ability rather than his or her content knowledge.

Other factors that influence the validity of formative assessments include the social and cultural factors that affect what goes on in the classroom itself. The motivation of the students and the value that they themselves place on learning and school can impact the validity of formative assessment. If students are not willing learners, it will be difficult for the assessment to provide valid information concerning the students' capabilities and thus allow us as teachers to use the data to impact learning.

## DETERMINING VALIDITY

In determining validity, three perspectives need to be considered: the form of the measure, the purpose of the assessment, and the population for which it is intended. Assessing the validity of an assessment is more than a simple question of "Is this test valid?" Validity is reported as a continuum, ranging from +1.00 to −1.00. A test is neither totally valid nor totally invalid; there are degrees of validity based upon the ability of the formative assessment to inform instruction and make decisions about whether or not a student has mastered a specific concept. Validity can be evaluated empirically as well as logically.

When assessed empirically, "it is very unusual for a validity coefficient to rise above 0.60, which is far from perfect prediction" (Assessment Oversight Policy Development Directorate 2007). There are several ways to estimate validity, including face validity, criterion-related validity, construct validity, and content validity. The following section will provide details about each of these methods for determining validity.

### Face Validity

Face validity is the simplest measure of validity. It is a matter of reviewing the assessment and determining at face value that the assessment aligns with the learning objectives it is designed to measure. Validity is assessed based on appearance. To strengthen the quality of this assessment of validity, it would be appropriate to share the formative assessment with colleagues who are also experts in the discipline the assessment is designed to measure. Check each element of the assessment to make sure that it is targeted for the specific learning objectives it is designed to address. Make sure that the assessment is not evaluating, instead, the student's reading ability when it is not a reading assessment.

## Criterion-Related Validity

Criterion-related validity is based upon the degree to which the assessment accurately predicts future performance in a real-life situation. For example, one of the measures of validity of the ACT test is based upon its ability to predict student college performance. This works with formative assessment as well; formative assessment is also a predictor of future performance. The validity of a formative assessment is based, in part, upon the measure's ability to predict a student's performance on a later summative assessment.

However, the validity of the measure as a formative assessment is also based upon the usability of the data obtained for addressing students' learning needs and improving their performance on a later summative assessment. You can assess the validity of the formative assessment by correlating the results from the measure with the students' later performance on a summative assessment. Establishing criterion-related validity is a good follow-up procedure when the formative assessment has been initially validated using only face validity.

## Construct Validity

Construct validity is an estimate of how much performance on the assessment varies due to changes in the construct. In this case the construct would be instruction. It is typically established using an experimental design, comparing performance between two groups, one that has received the instruction on which the assessment is based (the experimental group) and one that has not (the control group). If the group that has received the instruction performs better than the control group, the results show evidence of construct validity.

A pre/post test model can also be used to evaluate the validity of the assessment. This pre/post test approach would work well when validating a formative assessment. This is called an "intervention study." The formative assessment is given as a preassessment. Instruction is then delivered, and the same formative assessment is utilized to assess the students' ability to demonstrate mastery of the learning objective. If student scores are significantly higher on the postassessment, the test is considered valid.

## Content Validity

Content validity is the degree to which the formative assessment samples the content area associated with the learning goals the test is supposed to assess. A formative assessment is said to have content validity when it addresses all aspects of the objective it is designed to assess. Content validity relies on a logical analysis rather than an empirical analysis and is typically completed by a panel of content area experts. A simple review of the assessment developed, comparing it to the learning outcomes it is designed to evaluate, could be used to establish content validity for a formative assessment.

## RELIABILITY AND FORMATIVE ASSESSMENT

Reliability is an important measure of test quality and is of equal importance in terms of formative assessment. It is important that the tools we use to inform instruction provide consistent and reproducible information regarding student performance. These tools impact not only the quality of the information gathered but also the quality of feedback we are able to provide our students. If a formative assessment provides inconsistent data, it would be unethical to utilize the data to make inferences about the students' capabilities.

One of the greatest concerns, in terms of the reliability of formative assessment, is the accuracy of the teacher's interpretation of student responses (Nitko and Brookhart 2011). To enhance reliability, assessment should be based upon multiple questions and observation opportunities, and not just one instance. We need to utilize multiple assessments, triangulating the data to inform high-stakes decisions (National Center for Education Evaluation and Regional Assistance [NCEERA] 2009).

When seeking student responses orally, there should be sufficient wait time for the student to formulate a response. Many teachers provide the response themselves, if the response is not immediate. We need to give students enough time to think of an answer; this may take longer than we anticipate, and for some students it may take several minutes. It's important that we wait it out and not assume the student does not know the correct answer.

This relates to the issue of construct irrelevant variance. We need to remember that we are assessing the students' content knowledge rather than the speed with which they can generate a response. We assess recall speed by assessing automaticity. Automaticity is a factor we may want to

consider with certain foundational skills, such as the multiplication tables.

When using observation as a formative assessment tool, a wide spectrum of reasonable explanations should be used to interpret the behavior.
A systematic procedure should be implemented for observing student
behavior. This would include developing a record sheet where students'
responses and activities are recorded in a logical manner, allowing the
teacher to reflect on the observations at a later time.

The teacher's personal bias can also impact the reliability of the assessment. Our own personal beliefs about the students and their abilities may
negatively impact our interpretation of their responses. Again, this can be
negated by using a systematic procedure, such as a rubric, to evaluate
student responses. When we use a rubric, we should teach our students
about the rubric and how to use it to evaluate their own performance.
This will bring us back to the idea that formative assessment is a collaborative process, with the teacher and students working together to make
learning gains.

In addition to teacher error in interpretation of student responses,
outside issues may contribute to inconsistency in student performance
from one day to the next. The individual student's motivation, home life,
attitudes, careful reading of assessment directions, or test taking experience may impact the reliability of an assessment. If individual effort is
not applied when completing an assessment, the outcome of the assessment may be considered unreliable and invalid. This is a confounding
variable that needs to be considered, but in most cases, we have limited
control. This may be more a matter of developing a supportive learning
environment, but it is still an issue to consider.

## DETERMINING RELIABILITY

Reliability can be established by reviewing one of the three aspects of
reliability: equivalency, stability, and internal consistency. There are several methods for computing test reliability including test-retest reliability,
equivalency reliability, split-half reliability, stability reliability, internal
consistency, and interrater reliability. Each of these measures looks at one
of the three aspects of reliability. The ultimate determination of reliability
is the ability to repeat the assessment with limited change in the result,
except that which is due to the random influences that naturally occur
with testing.

How reliability is estimated depends on the reason that is most likely
to cause inconsistency in the results from a given assessment (Cortina
1993). If the passage of time is believed to be an issue, then a model using
test-retest would be an appropriate measure. If inconsistency is believed
to be due to interaction between questions within the assessment, or an

interaction between the students and the assessment, then internal consistency would be an appropriate measure. In the following section we will review several options to establish the reliability of a formative assessment.

### Equivalency Reliability

Equivalency reliability compares the results of one assessment to the results of a similar assessment designed to assess the same learning outcomes. It is calculated using a correlation measure comparing scores achieved by the same or similar group of students. Since they are designed to measure the same constructs, the scores obtained should be similar. It is difficult to construct two assessments that are essentially equivalent, but when given the opportunity it can be a valuable tool to establish reliability.

### Test-Retest Reliability

Test-retest reliability is a measure of stability, addressing the degree to which scores are consistent over time. If an assessment is repeatedly administered, there should be little variance except for that which would normally, randomly occur. This can easily be evaluated by having students complete the assessment twice over an extended period of time. Issues arise when students remember the assessment and either remember the correct responses from their previous experience or have learned new information related to the assessment. If time is too extended, changes in student scores may also be due to increased maturity.

### Internal Consistency

Internal consistency looks at the correlation between the questions that make up an assessment. It looks at the degree that questions measure the same learning objectives. When evaluating the internal consistency, the results for each question are compared first to each other and then to the overall score achieved on the assessment. If students score similarly on questions designed to assess the same outcome, the test is deemed reliable. The responses are said to have a high correlation.

A split half estimate may be used by dividing the test into two parts. For example, the results from all the odd-numbered questions can be compared with the results from all the even-numbered questions. The scores from the two halves can then be correlated, providing an empirical score of the test's reliability.

*Interrater Reliability*

Interrater reliability is another form of equivalency reliability. In terms of formative assessment, the equivalency between those who score and interpret the assessment is of great importance. When multiple individuals are observing and scoring a behavior, artifact, or student response, the scorers should agree on what constitutes the presence or absence of an indicator that demonstrates student ability. Determining interrater reliability is a simple equation:

# of agreements / # of opportunities for agreement M 100

This will result in a percentage. If evaluators agreed 35 times out of a possible 50 opportunities (i.e., 50 unique observations, interpretations, or ratings), then they would be in agreement 70% of the time (35/50 = 0.70 M 100 = 70%).

## FORMATIVE ASSESSMENT METHODS FOR ENSURING VALIDITY AND RELIABILITY

Formative assessment is a process, not a single assessment. Within that process, assessments are utilized to gather data that will help inform teaching practices and provide students with valid feedback that can be used by them to improve their own performance. As indicated by the discussion in this chapter regarding validity and reliability, it is important that the information gathered from these assessments be reliable and valid to the greatest degree possible. Instructionally, inaccurate information will likely damage the teacher-student relationship and will likely not improve student performance.

Taking the time to measure the validity and reliability of the measures used in formative assessment should play a key role in the formative assessment process you are implementing in your classroom. As a classroom teacher, you are not likely to have the resources at hand to do an in-depth, detailed research analysis of each of the assessments you employ in your classroom. Some districts have gone to the level of implementing computer-based, short-cycle assessments that can be used to support formative assessment using measures that have established reliability and validity.

The individual educator can, in many cases, develop a procedure for implementing short, quick teacher-created formative assessments that are valid and reliable. Following are procedures that you should consider implementing in your formative assessment process to strengthen the validity and reliability of the assessments you create and use to inform instruction.

*Supporting Content Validity*

As you design a formative assessment, first consider the domain in which the objectives you will be assessing lie. There are three fundamental domains addressed in educational activities (Bloom 1956): cognitive, affective, and psychomotor. For the assessment to be valid there needs to be a clear alignment between the domain and the assessment utilized.

The cognitive domain focuses on an individual's intellectual abilities. Within the cognitive domain, Bloom (1956) identified six levels of cognitive difficulty: knowledge, comprehension, application, analysis, synthesis, and evaluation. These were revised by Lorin Anderson in the mid 1990s (Pohl 2000), changing the names from nouns to verbs and reordering the last two levels: remembering, understanding, applying, analyzing, evaluating, and creating.

Within the affective domain, Bloom associated five emotional behaviors: receiving phenomena, responding to phenomena, valuing, organization, and internalizing values. The affective domain addresses the emotions that a student experiences toward specific learning experiences. The psychomotor domain refers to the basic motor skills and coordination associated with physical movement. Simpson (1972) identified seven categories to support this domain: perception, set, guided response, mechanism, complex overt response, adaptation, and origination.

The cognitive and psychomotor domains are the ones that are most likely to be addressed using formative assessment procedures, although they can all be assessed formatively. To determine the associated domain, consider the specific behavior required by the learning objective. Consider what the students need to be able to do in order to exhibit the skill. Match the verb included in the objective to the activity required in the assessment. If the objective requires the students to identify something, a simple matching or multiple choice test will suffice. If an objective requires the students to create something, then the assessment needs to have students complete a hands-on project in which they create.

With a formative assessment you may have the student complete indicators that will not assess their ability to meet the whole intent of the standard but will support their learning as they develop the skill necessary to do so. For example, if the learning standard states, "With guidance and support from adults, produce writing in which the development and organization are appropriate to task and purpose" (CCSS.ELA-Literacy.W.3.4), you may ask the students to do a free-write in which they describe a photograph of a cultural festival. This formative assessment would encompass only a small portion of the intent of the standard, but it would let the teacher assess the student's ability to write a description, and help the teacher use that information to build the student's skill to the point where he or she will meet the entire intent of the standard.

To strengthen the validity assessments that are used formatively, we need to make sure that the learning goals and objectives the assessment is designed to measure are clearly defined. To support this, you can utilize the appropriate content standards to help delineate and define the learning objectives. These may include national content standards, state standards, and the Common Core State Standards (CCSS). Ideally, using the appropriate standards as a guide, you can break down each learning outcome to the operational level. Also consider the indicators that make up the objective.

For example, consider the indicators associated with the objective "Students will be able to compare and contrast political ideologies." You would need to define "competence" in terms of this objective and what "competence" would look like behaviorally. You might include the political ideologies to be addressed, goals vs. methods employed within each ideology, the form of government supported by each ideology, countries currently supporting each ideology, the impact on the national and international economy, and so on. Multiple factors impact each learning objective, and we need to consider the facets that will need to be observed to demonstrate mastery by the student.

We need to make sure formative assessments address the foundational knowledge and skills that will support students as they continue in their study of the content. Checklists can be utilized that clearly identify the indicators that the learner will demonstrate as he or she develops mastery of the learning outcome. After developing an assessment, seek feedback from colleagues and even students. Feedback from parties less vested in the instrument will allow you to refine the assessment and improve its overall validity.

*Supporting Stability Reliability*

To ensure the reliability of the measures you create or implement, make sure that you have sufficient questions to adequately assess achievement of each of the core learning objectives you are assessing. As a general guideline, include three or more questions or items for each objective (Garies and Grant 2008). With formative assessment, these may take the form of different measures to be used during instruction. You could include a free-write, a discussion, and a learning activity, all designed to assess student progress with the same learning outcome.

As you design a unit of instruction, map specific formative assessments to each learning objective that will be addressed and assessed in the unit. Make sure that you have identified multiple opportunities to assess individual student performance on each of the core competencies you will be teaching.

As you develop assessments to be used formatively, proofread each assessment (including individual test questions, prompts, and directions) for errors, cultural biases, and clarity. Be consistent in your approach and make sure that students have the opportunity to become comfortable with your assessment practices. Develop a template for each type of formative assessment you will implement. For example, consider the format you will use when having the students complete free-writes. You could determine that each free-write will take five to ten minutes to complete and will be based upon a current issue the class is discussing.

Finally, as you develop the assessments, consider the grading criteria and rubrics you will use to score the assessments. Grading criteria will be the greatest offender in terms of interrater reliability, or differences in scoring by two or more individuals. Without a well-written scoring guide, it is difficult to maintain consistency when grading student responses. The behavioral descriptors associated with each criterion and performance level need to be clearly defined and understood in order for there to be consistency in the evaluation of student responses.

Behavioral descriptors will also impact intra-rater reliability — scoring done by just one individual. We tend to think, "I'm the teacher, and I will be scoring every item and observation." However, as much as we may think of our own objectivity, it is easy to score differently based upon who the student is who completed the task and our own biases concerning his or her skills and abilities. Our own emotional attitude at the time we are grading can interfere with our ability to objectively score student work. Clear, descriptive criteria are necessary to ensure reliability and consistency when scoring student responses.

Using a rubric to score performance-based or authentic assessments increases the reliability of the assessment. To improve the reliability of rubrics, consider the following strategies (Jonsson and Svingby 2007). First, provide strict guidelines that detail the expectations for student work in terms of the assessment. The criteria used in the rubric should be selected carefully, ensuring that they support the learning objectives being assessed.

Second, consider utilizing analytic rubrics rather than holistic rubrics that are specific to the assessment being scored. An analytic rubric is used to score each individual characteristic or indicator related to the assessment. A holistic rubric looks at the student product from a holistic perspective, looking at student performance on various criteria with a broader, less focused lens. Additionally, if you provide examples that demonstrate the various performance levels described in the rubric, reliability will be further improved as well.

Finally, a rubric that includes only two performance levels, "meets outcome" or "doesn't meet outcome," is much easier to score and has far greater reliability than a rubric that includes four or more performance levels. When designed with only two performance levels, the rubric becomes more of a checklist, in which you just verify that the student has met the indicator associated with the learning objective or that the student needs further instruction. This simplified form has high reliability and is a quick, useful tool to track student performance.

## CONCLUSION

Just as with all assessment practices, the validity and reliability of the assessment determines the quality of the information that will be obtained from the measure. Since the intent of formative assessments is to inform instruction and support the learning process, the validity and reliability of these assessments are of even greater importance.

As the teacher, you need to have a clear understanding of your students' skills and abilities, using these as benchmarks as you help students grow in those skills and abilities. While you may not be able to conduct a full analysis of the validity or reliability of the measure to be used, it is important that you make every effort to develop formative assessments that are valid and reliable.

At a minimum, implement face validity, working with your colleagues to make sure that the assessments utilized assess the identified learning outcomes. Then, over time, track student data, comparing results and making sure that the assessment outcomes indicate validity and reliability. The assessments and the scoring measures you will use to evaluate student performance should be based on the standards and learning objectives they are designed to evaluate. Work to provide clear directions and well-detailed scoring rubrics or checklists. Align the assessment to the domain addressed by the objective. Additionally, take the time to break the learning outcome down to the specific indicators that together make up the learning outcome.

Finally, for formative assessment to be effective and valid, the classroom learning environment must be supportive and collaborative. The feedback given to students must be specific and informative, providing them with enough information so that they can also work to improve their performance.

Formative assessment is truly a collaboration between the teacher and the students. To be effective, there must be trust between teacher and students, and all involved need to be motivated with a desire to learn and grow as a team. The classroom climate determines the validity and reliability of formative assessments, just as much as the assessment itself does.

# FOUR

## Assignments and Assessments

Teachers require students to complete learning activities, assignments, and summative assessments as part of the instructional and grading process. Unfortunately, usually the outcomes of these activities are only recorded in the grade book. The learning data that could be gained from these common tools are seldom mined.

What the teacher could learn about what the students know, understand, and are able to do through those assignments and assessments is lost. Data from these tools are seldom used to inform instruction and support further student learning. They are simply grades to be entered into the grade book. In this chapter we will discuss the use of assignments and summative assessments as tools to support formative assessment.

### GATHERING DATA FOR FORMATIVE ASSESSMENT PURPOSES

Formative assessment does not need to include out-of-the-ordinary activities. We can employ the same tools we already use daily as formative assessment tools. To be used formatively, assignments and assessments need to be tied to specific learning outcomes. Prior to giving an assignment or delivering an assessment, it should be determined if we will use the data formatively.

Once you've determined that an activity will be used as a formative assessment, outline the objectives that you will assess through this activity. Identify the characteristics you will be able to observe through the assignment that will inform you of the students' current skill with the objective you've identified. For example, you could use lab reports from science class to assess their ability to "follow precisely a multistep procedure when carrying out experiments, taking measurements, or perform-ing technical tasks" (CCSS.ELA-Literacy.RST.6-8.3.).

To use the lab report to assess this Common Core State Standard, you might monitor the degree to which students followed the process. You might look at the step-by-step process used in completing the lab report, and check the accuracy of the methods and measures employed in the lab. Your focus would be on the procedure and accuracy of the report. While you may want students to demonstrate other skills in the report in terms of the grade you will assign, for formative assessment purposes you would only focus on the details outlined by the learning outcome for which you are gathering data.

Additionally, assignments designed for grading purposes should not be your only sources for formative data. It is important that multiple measures be used to track student learning for the purposes of instruc-tion. Rather than basing a student's success or failure on one score, the purpose of formative assessment requires us to provide for multiple checkpoints. These checkpoints will allow us to better meet the students' learning needs rather than judge their ability to perform.

A system must be in place to record and track the data obtained at each checkpoint, whether that checkpoint is an item used for grading purposes or a measure that is specifically for formative assessment pur-poses. Tracking needs to be more than recording the percentage a student gets correct on an assessment.

It is important that information be gathered that will allow you to help students develop problem-solving strategies and ways of thinking that will allow them to implement those skills and strategies. To do this, you need to know how the students are currently approaching the content to be learned. It's important to know their weaknesses and strengths. You also need to be able to identify holes in your students' understanding and the methods that they currently employ to learn and to demonstrate their learning.

If you use rubrics to grade assignments, you will be able to score subjective activities with a degree of objectivity. You will also be able to quickly obtain more detail regarding student performance and the qual-ity of that performance. The rubric needs to be well defined, providing you with an accurate description that can then be applied to the students' level of performance.

You can even use a simple rubric to score students' math work: 3 points if the students show their work and arrive at the correct answer, 2 points if the students show their work but make a computational error, 1 point if the students arrive at the correct answer but do not show their work, and 0 points if the students do not show their work and have an incorrect answer. A scoring rubric, whether it is a simple rubric as de-scribed here or something more complex, like a six-trait writing rubric, can provide you with specific information about student skills that need more support or instruction.

Performance-based learning activities and assignments are especially valuable to the formative assessment process. These types of assignments lend themselves to multiple checkpoints and monitoring of student progress. At each point, there is opportunity for you to provide the students with feedback on their performance.

The value of performance-based activities can be extended when feedback is also provided at the time a final grade is assigned to the project. At this point you can opt to give students the option of redoing or revising the project or product based on your feedback, for full or partial credit—thus hitting the reset button and allowing students to go back and relearn the skill or concept that was addressed by the assignment.

## USING SUMMATIVE ASSESSMENTS FORMATIVELY

Traditionally, evaluation of student learning is put off until the end of a unit, too late to inform instructional decisions so that student learning can be supported based on the findings. Additionally, chapter tests and unit assessments are typically graded and thus can be perceived by students to be threatening. This fear of failure can impact the reliability of the results from graded assessments. Summative assessments can be used formatively if they are designed appropriately and if you have worked to develop a learning environment that is supportive. Ideally the learning environment needs to be one where failure is not feared but is seen as a means to learning.

The timing of the assessment is key to using a summative assessment formatively. Summative assessments are summative because they are a student's last chance to work with this information. They primarily serve to compare and judge a student's ability to perform at a given point in time. The formative assessment process, instead, tries "to find the optimal conditions for making visible a young child's understanding in order to enhance it" (Honey 2007).

Formative assessment looks beyond right and wrong answers to the strategies used by students to problem solve, address an issue, or arrive at an answer. In order to use assignments or summative assessments to inform the formative assessment process, procedures need to be put in place that allow you to see the strategies the student uses to arrive at an answer, right or wrong. If we allow the learning to flow into the next unit, or if we allow students and the instructor to revisit the information, it becomes formative, and students get to hit the reset button and try again.

Another important factor is the opportunity for students to revise their work. Just as you can allow students to revise assignments based on teacher feedback, the same philosophy can be applied to tests. We can let students defend their incorrect responses. If they can provide additional information that supports the answer they give to a question, you could award students partial credit for that question. While students gather the information to defend their answers, they will learn the material in greater depth. This turns an assessment into a learning opportunity and not just a grade.

We need to change our perspective and see assessment as a tool to support learning, not just as a means to assign a grade. Assignments and learning activities are valuable tools for formative assessment. The information gleaned from those activities can be applied to the instructional process. We can use our findings to change instruction and provide students with direct, specific feedback to improve their performance.

To do this with a summative assessment, we should follow up the assessment with opportunities for students to demonstrate their improvement in future assignments, activities, and assessments. We also need to identify content objectives that flow through to the next unit, and we need to focus on opportunities to reteach or reinforce those skills.

Finally, the information learned about the student must be used to inform instruction so that teaching methods and materials that are designed to help each student develop the skills they need to be successful academically can be implemented. The data from these assessments should be used to revise instruction and enhance student achievement.

We can use our summative evaluations formatively by taking the results and using that information to develop instruction that will work to improve student outcomes, either through reteaching information on which students performed poorly or by changing how the information will be delivered in future classes.

## DOCUMENTING

The value of a well-designed assignment or summative assessment to the formative assessment process is only as good as the documentation. In evaluating student work for the purpose of formative assessment, attention must be paid to individual performance on the key learning outcomes that the formative assessment process is focused on. Documentation must go beyond identifying learning outcomes the students have mastered. Evidence must also be collected regarding the students' strengths and weaknesses. Time should to be taken to identify specific subskills related to each learning outcome. Student performance related to these subskills can also be assessed.

The attitude to be applied in formative assessment is one of "finding out." The purpose in evaluating data for formative purposes is one of figuring out what is going on. We work to understand the students' intent with a particular response—trying to understand for ourselves where students are in terms of learning the content, rather than becoming distracted by confounding variables that interfere with our ability to understand their work.

The focus is on the learning outcomes, not on the student's writing ability, attitude, behavior, or ability to submit work on time. Factors such as these frequently interfere with the quality of documentation of student performance. Student work is marked down because the assignment is submitted late or is poorly written.

Bias can also interfere with the scoring of student work. A student who is identified as a "problem student" may receive a score that is lower than deserved. And a student who is known as a "good student" may receive a score that is higher than deserved.

Formative assessments help the teacher understand the current skill level of the student or class, and determine whether or not the students are "ready" to move forward. They allow you, as the teacher, to make course corrections. You may end up reteaching certain concepts, clarifying issues, or making sure the connection between the previous skills and concepts are clear as they relate to the new information. Formative assessments give the teacher the opportunity to analyze the progress of the students. And it gives them the opportunity to adjust their teaching so that more students reach proficiency.

## KNOW, UNDERSTAND, AND DO: KUD

KUD is an acronym utilized in backward design. It stands for three types of objectives: Know, Understand, and Do. As we design a unit we need to answer the question "What do we want our students to know, understand, and be able to do?" When using summative assessments to support the learning of students in the next unit, our attention should be focused on the knowledge, understanding, and skills the students will need to retain and be able to apply, to be successful as they progress to the next leve!.

It is important to identify the knowledge level of information students need to know well. Identify the facts, vocabulary, and other concrete pieces of information such as dates, places, and examples that they will need to know. A popular quote, attributed to Carol Ann Tomlinson (Imbeau 2012), reads as follows, "The 'know' is massively forgettable unless you hook it to understanding. Teaching facts in isolation is like trying to pump water uphill." So, we need to go beyond knowledge.

Students also need to understand the relevance and the application of the knowledge level objectives we've identified. Being able to transfer the knowledge to another situation is evidence of the students' level of understanding (or lack of it).

Finally, we need to know the skills students will need to be "able to do." We need to consider the skills that they will need to apply as the result of instruction. In addition to content specific skills in which students are able to apply knowledge they have mastered to problem solving or research, we need to address other learning skills. These skills may include thinking skills such as analyzing, evaluating, and synthesizing. They may also include planning skills, independent learning skills, or skills to set and follow criteria.

The process of being able to identify the information that we draw from an assessment to use formatively would be greatly enhanced if we took KUD into consideration during the development of instruction. As we design our assessments we need to write them so that they help us evaluate whether or not our students achieved what we want them to know, understand, and be able to do. We need to emphasize the transferability of knowledge. Can our students transfer what they have learned to another content area, a different problem or related activity, or another situation?

Many times teachers are accused of not teaching students a particular concept or skill, when in reality the problem isn't that it wasn't taught. The problem often is that the students were unable to transfer the knowledge to a different environment. Many math teachers have taught their students the metric system in mathematics, and then find that those students claim no knowledge of metrics when in their science class. We need to help them make the connection that, yes, mathematics, science, English, history, and other content areas are related and one does transfer to the other.

## INFORMING FUTURE INSTRUCTION

Using backward design and applying the concepts of differentiated instruction to our teaching and the summative assessments we give provides a way of thinking about the classroom that focuses on student learning. Our goals are those of honoring each student's learning needs and maximizing each student's learning capacity while developing a solid community of learners. Formative assessment is integral to that perspective.

The purpose of formative assessment is to inform future instruction. It's a matter of using formative assessment to identifying those learning needs and addressing them in our future instruction. In the case of using summative assessment to support the formative assessment process, we need to identify factors made evident from that assessment that can be used to identify gaps in the students' learning. With that knowledge, we can then design instruction that will help students close or bridge those gaps.

Summative assessments can provide direction for the next unit you have designed and help you clarify the essential questions and big ideas that you feel are important for all students to learn, regardless of their learning ability or interest. Utilize the summative assessment to measure not only recall but also the depth and level of understanding. We can also use them to assess the students' ability to communicate what was learned. Additionally, we can assess the degree to which students can transfer what was learned to a more difficult problem or issue or to a different setting.

Instruction can and should be differentiated in three different areas: content, process, and product. Likewise the summative assessments we employ can also be differentiated for content, process, and product. By differentiating assessment and incorporating means to differentiate content, process, and product in our assessments, we can learn more about the students' depth of understanding and the skills and abilities they are able to apply.

Content is the basis of instruction and the primary focus of most of our teaching. We can vary our content to meet the needs of our students. For instruction this means that lower-level students may need a more simplified content, and higher-level students may need more complex content. We can teach and assess most content at multiple levels. You could teach a unit on the Oregon Trail in the early primary grades, middle school, and the high school level, but the complexity and depth of that content would probably vary. That variance can be applied to assessment.

We can vary process by designing assessments to address a student's readiness needs, thus assessing his or her content knowledge rather than reading ability. This can be done by varying the process we use to assess the content. We could adjust the complexity of the reading material included in the test, providing a simplified vocabulary or format. We could choose to make an audio recording of the assessment questions, so a student can listen to the questions rather than read them. Or, we could have a student respond verbally rather than in writing.

Finally, we can vary the product submitted by students to demonstrate their learning. We could use a choice board where students can select the product they will submit to demonstrate their learning. Students could demonstrate their ability to "distinguish among facts, reasoned judgment based on research findings, and speculation in a text" (CCSS.ELA-Literacy.RST.6-8.8), by writing a paper, developing and delivering a presentation, creating a documentary, or designing an experiment or research study.

We can create opportunities to vary the product submitted based upon their interests, learning style, or learner readiness. It's okay to require a different product from higher-, middle-, and lower-level students. There are many ways to demonstrate understanding of a concept, and they do not need to be of equal difficulty. But they do all need to demonstrate understanding of the concept being assessed.

## CONCEPTS THAT THREAD THROUGH THE CURRICULUM

By planning assessments before planning lessons, we will be able to identify key learning outcomes, determine appropriate places and times to assess, and find effective ways to assess, matching the assessment to the desired objective. We need to take into account what we want the students to be able to do with the information.

If simple recall and the ability to select is enough, a multiple choice assessment is appropriate. But if the ability to perform a specific skill is needed, a multiple choice assessment is not appropriate. Just as you wouldn't give a figure skater a multiple choice test to assess their ability to skate, you should not use a multiple choice assessment to measure a performance skill. We need to make sure we are assessing the desired learning.

For all content areas there are concepts that flow through the entire domain. In math, students apply basic arithmetic skills on through the highest levels of mathematics. In English, students apply basic grammar skills, sentence structure, and the concept of a main idea in everything they write. The same is true of science, history, physical education, art, and music: there are concepts that flow from the most basic levels to the highest. Also within each domain there are skills, factual pieces of knowledge, and key understandings that thread through the curriculum.

Summative assessments can be used to assess these skills as well as others that thread through the curriculum. If we use summative assessments to evaluate those skills that students must transfer to the next unit in order to be successful, we can use our findings to design instruction that will help students learn the key concepts they have yet to master. By combining summative assessment from previous learning opportunities and formative assessment with the design of instruction, we will be able to better ensure the success of all students.

## CONCLUSION

Summative assessments can be used for what is traditionally its primary purpose: grading and formal evaluation. When designed appropriately, however, they can also be used to support the formative assessment process. Summative assessments can provide feedback regarding the success of the instruction that was implemented, as well as the continued learning needs of the student. If the results of the assessment are used to improve instruction or to reteach concepts, it is being used as a formative assessment as well as a summative assessment.

Rather than just looking at the scores and moving on to the next unit, we need to take a moment and make sure there are no foundational skills or concepts that we need to take the time to reteach. We need to use everything we do in class as a tool to improve instruction. Summative assessment can be one of those tools.

# FIVE

# Preassessments

Formative assessment begins before you enter the classroom and continues on through pretesting and other diagnostic-type assessments that might be conducted to determine where students are in their readiness to learn the content addressing these questions: (1) What prior knowledge or content knowledge do they already possess? and (2) Do they have the prerequisite skills to learn the content? Additionally, preassessments provide a wonderful tool to get to know our students, and many times they help us identify students' strengths and weaknesses as learners.

We can learn more about a variety of factors that influence the teaching and learning process, including creativity; critical thinking abilities; students' ability to transfer knowledge, skills, and information to other situations and topics; prior experience; learning preferences such as group vs. independent learning; and interpersonal skills.

The list could go on and on—but most importantly, we need to find out about our students. What multiple intelligences come to the forefront for a particular student or class? Are there kinesthetic learners in the class who need to move around? Are they sensing (attending more to the information that comes in through the five senses) or intuitive (responding more to the patterns and possibilities they perceive)? We can plan to their strengths in our instruction, and we can design activities to build strengths where there is weakness.

Using preassessment findings, we can determine if we need to design several entry points in a given lesson for students, allowing for the diversity that exists in the classroom in terms of learning ability, aptitude, and interest. As the teacher, you can use this data to help students begin to learn at a level that will challenge them, but also at a point where they are prepared to succeed. We can also use this data to gain an understanding of the wide variety of interests that are present in our class and to frame the lessons we design.

Rather than designing instruction based upon the needs of the students, often teachers let the textbook determine their curriculum. Too many times our preparation for teaching a particular course begins and ends with the textbook. At times we rely far too heavily on the information contained within the textbook and its organization to determine how and what we teach, even given the increased focus on standards in the past several decades.

Ideally, we should focus more specifically on the needs of our students, using preassessments to identify student characteristics and interests, as well as content preparation, to inform lesson planning and the selection of instructional strategies and learning activities. We need to stop, look, and listen to our students. We need to take the time to conduct a needs assessment to determine where our students are in their learning.

With the increasingly diverse population present in our classrooms, it is even more important that we plan curriculum and instruction systematically and use data to inform the development of instruction. We know that within each class, even tracked classes, there will be a wide range of needs. We must be prepared to address those needs.

When we take the time to find out about where students are with a given topic we can use this information to compress instruction for some or all students, allowing students to move more quickly or at a higher level through the content, or slowing things down when students need more time and instruction to fully understand the content. Many times, we lull our students into a state of complacency when we teach the same content over and over.

For example, if you were to examine the typical textbook for fifth-, sixth-, seventh-, and eighth-grade general math, you would find that the texts cover the same content through most of the book, with very little difference, with the only new material being introduced in the last few chapters of the text. To compound this issue, most teachers seldom reach those final chapters, so the students spend a great deal of time relearning the addition and subtraction of three-digit decimals over and over during these grades.

Repetition is good, but we don't want to bore them into complacency. Consider also the number of students who become behavior issues in the classroom because they are bored. We can use our preassessment information to determine if we can teach the class as a whole group or if we need to create two or three entry points for students, differentiating instruction and allowing them to work at a level that is appropriate for them.

To perform preassessment, it is not necessary to complete a formalized assessment. Preassessments do not necessarily need to be graded and given a score. Many times opening our eyes and ears is enough.

Sometimes we just need to take the time to notice and record our observations. It's important that data from preassessments be gathered and recorded. They will provide a baseline set of data that can be used to track not only student performance, but also student gains. They will also help us gain a clear understanding of our students and their capabilities, allowing us to make better use of the teaching time available.

Preassessments are the foundational tool for completing a needs assessment. They can tell us more about our students than their knowledge of the content, if we take the time to complete the assessment and make sense of what we've learned. While the most common form of preassessment is the paper-and-pencil quiz, there are many tools we can use. In this chapter, we will discuss how to conduct a needs assessment in greater detail, and then we will review a variety of assessments that you can use to perform a needs analysis prior to beginning instruction.

## NEEDS ASSESSMENT

Preassessments are used in conducting a needs analysis to identify where our students are in meeting the standards, the prior knowledge related to the content, and their readiness to move forward with new content. One of the biggest mistakes that designers, teachers, and educators make is assuming that instruction is the solution to all performance problems. Sometimes additional supports, other than instruction, are needed to help students overcome performance issues such as reading level, learning disabilities, or physical handicaps.

In completing a full needs analysis you need to evaluate the learning environment, student preparation and readiness, and the content being taught. We tend to think that if it's in the text, we have to teach it. Frequently that is impossible and unnecessary. The amount of content in many texts is so voluminous that it would be impossible to address all of the text with any degree of detail or depth. Secondly, most curricula and the standards they address are designed to be repetitive, except for higher-level classes.

Many times, students come to our classes with foundational knowledge that is simply retaught rather than being mined and built upon. Rather than accepting at face value that we need to teach everything contained within a text, covering the material, we need to carefully select the content that the students in our current class need, prioritizing what we teach and teaching some things in greater depth and others in greater breadth. The idea behind a needs analysis is to determine the current conditions ("what is") and comparing it to where our students "ought to be."

*Identify the Learning Goals*

In completing a needs assessment, first we identify the learning goals to be addressed in a specific unit of instruction. Second, we assess where our students are in terms of achieving these goals—finding out if there really is a need. Have students already achieved these goals? Are they ready to move on? Or do they need additional instruction or supports to help them achieve the learning goals identified? What gaps exist in terms of meeting the learning goals?

Once we've identified the gaps, we need to prioritize them and teach the most important or foundational skills and concepts first. If students do not have the foundational knowledge required to learn the new content, then they are not likely to be successful in gaining higher skills and levels of critical thinking (e.g., multiplication tables, how to write a sentence, scientific method).

Yes, it would be nice if students achieved every learning goal identified, but we need to prioritize and consider the consequences if students do not achieve certain learning goals. Some learning goals are in the "nice to know" category, and others truly are key to their future understanding of the content. Typically, standards identified by the states and professional organizations do a good job of identifying that foundational knowledge. It's up to the teacher to identify the next level of knowledge and skills, which will allow the student to become engaged and involved in the content area.

*Evaluate the Learners*

Consider the learners' individual characteristics. Students will likely be similar in some areas. Being from the same or similar age groups, they are likely to be alike developmentally and in their ability to process information. Differences will exist, however, in terms of IQ, cognitive styles, gender, ethnicity, and prior learning. In terms of needs assessment, this is where preassessments fit. We can use the preassessment tools described later on in this chapter to determine where students are in relation to the learning goals we've identified, as well as the learner characteristics that are most important to our instruction and in our classroom.

We need to be aware of our students, their similarities and differences, their learning characteristics and sensory capacities. A wide variety of things, internal and external to the classroom, have an impact on students and their ability to learn.

*Evaluate the Task*

As we review our learning goals, we need to be aware of the types of learning we are asking students to achieve. Is the focus on declarative knowledge such as might be found in a history class or more procedural knowledge like that found in a math class? We need to anticipate our learners' needs and identify the cognitive strategies and psychomotor skills that we will need to teach students so they can more easily assimilate the learning. We need to consider whether we will be teaching things that are more attitudinal or affective. Analyze the prerequisites that students will need in order to learn the content or concept, or to complete the task.

By performing a needs analysis prior to beginning instruction, we can design instruction that moves students forward rather than holding them back.

## PREASSESSMENT TOOLS

Key to using preassessments effectively and efficiently in instruction is developing methods to easily record and analyze the data obtained. If it's not quick and easy, you are less likely to use the information gained. This section details a number of preassessments that can effectively and efficiently be implemented in the classroom and utilized to support student learning and the design of instruction.

### Frayer Diagram

A Frayer diagram is a tool you can use to determine students' knowledge of various concepts and their interrelationships. With a Frayer diagram, students map a concept, providing a definition and identifying key characteristics. Additionally, they make a brief list of examples of the concept and then on the opposite side list nonexamples. By having the students list both examples and nonexamples, you will be able to more accurately assess their understanding of the scope of the concept. You might have students develop a Frayer diagram for mammals.

Again, you would look at the accuracy and depth of the responses, identifying holes in the students' understanding of the concept. This assessment will allow you to quickly identify those students who do not have a clear understanding of the concept being addressed. Key in this assessment is the students' ability to identify both examples and nonexamples, clearly delineating the difference between them.

In examining student response, pay particular attention to the examples and nonexamples identified. Consider the types of examples presented. Does the student include only those examples that are most commonly known and clearly identified? Or does the student include lesser-known examples that are more difficult to identify? Do the examples cover a wide spectrum of possibilities, or is it a more focused list addressing only a narrow portion of the definition? Also examine the nonexam-

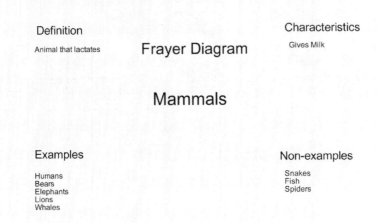

**Figure 5.1.   Frayer Diagram on Mammals**

ples. Are the nonexamples easily differentiated from the examples? Are they so far out that they could be easily identified as nonexamples? Or are the nonexamples closely related to the concept and difficult to identify as nonexamples?

Again, organize student responses by the degree of understanding. If a student only identifies examples and nonexamples that are easy to identify, he or she likely has a weaker understanding than a student who can identify a greater breadth of examples and nonexamples more closely related to the concept. Work with the student to develop a broader understanding of the concept and develop his or her skill in finding characteristics that help identify examples and nonexamples of the concept.

For example, in the Frayer diagram provided above, students who listed examples of a diverse range of mammals (there are over five thousand species of living mammals) would have a greater understanding of the concept. This would be particularly true if they were able to identify the distinguishing characteristics that determine if a species is mammalian (mammals have hair, are warm-blooded, and produce milk).

A student who could only name easily identified mammals (humans, cows, goats) and nonexamples (fly, spider, snake) would demonstrate a more limited understanding of the concept. Activities should be developed that give these students a broader understanding of the concept and the difference between this concept and other closely related concepts, such as the difference between mammals and reptiles.

## Pretest

The traditional pretest also works well as a preassessment. It can be as simple as giving a multiple choice or short-answer assessment that addresses the key concepts to be covered in a unit or prior knowledge students should have mastered before studying the new content. A colleague who taught middle school math would frequently test students over those basic skills that are repeated in general math classes at the fifth-, sixth-, seventh-, and eighth-grade levels. This allowed her to focus on the concepts that students had not retained, or not transferred to her math class, early in the school year and then move on to new concepts quickly, rather than repeating content the students had already mastered.

Pretests on later units allowed her to group students according to their level of mastery. This allowed her to challenge students who had already mastered the content at grade level, moving them into more difficult material. This also allowed her to design instructional supports for students who were working below grade level.

The primary purpose of a pretest is to determine if the students have the foundational knowledge necessary to learn the new information or the current capability with the content to be taught. Pretests, as well as other preassessments, provide a baseline. Pretests, however, are usually more easily quantified. This baseline can be used to track student growth throughout the school year. Pretests also allow you to identify the students' level of preparedness.

We need to review the results of these assessments purposefully, identifying the skills and knowledge that are foundational to learning the content to be taught. If students lack primary skills or knowledge important to future success with the content, you will need to stop and take the time to teach those foundations. You may need to differentiate instruction based upon the students' readiness, addressing the needs of those who are missing the key pieces as well as the needs of those who already have a good knowledge base in terms of the content to be taught.

## Knowledge Survey

Similar to pretests, a knowledge survey allows you to determine, quickly and efficiently, where students are in their knowledge of the content. Surveys, however, are more indicative of perception rather than demonstration of actual knowledge. A knowledge survey consists of statements on which students self-evaluate using a Likert scale. For example, a statement might read, "I can describe the water cycle accurately." Students would be asked to evaluate themselves on a five-point scale from "strongly agree" to "strongly disagree." We can vary the scale to include options such as "never" to "always" or "I am well prepared" to "I am not prepared."

The data can easily be organized, identifying those who "strongly agree" or "agree" and others who "strongly disagree" or "disagree" with the statements. We can track student responses, identifying those students who are confident in terms of the content to be learned versus those who do not feel well prepared. We need to remember this is self-report information, which means that accuracy of the responses may be questionable, but generally student responses will give us an idea of what students already know and what they are comfortable with.

### Poster/Artifact Walk

The poster/artifact walk allows the students to explore, beforehand, what they will learn. It whets their appetite and gives them an opportunity to share with you what they already know about a subject. The poster/artifact walk can be created entirely by the teacher, or it can be developed in collaboration with the students. Post pictures, quotes, and artifacts about the unit to be studied around the classroom. Then have the students write down what they know and ideas they have about the items posted and share them with the class. This last stage can be completed as a whole group activity or on an individual basis.

You could combine this with the KWL assessment, using the images and artifacts to help trigger the students' memories of what they already know, perhaps engaging their interest, and helping students identify things they would like to learn about the content. Using the visual display as a cue to enhance student recall, you will be able to better identify what they know by helping them more readily draw that knowledge from their long-term memories. Alone, or in combination with KWL, this assessment will provide you with information that can be utilized to focus instruction on specific areas in which the students need support or extended information.

Again, be aware of the level of the understanding of the content and the interrelationships of the various concepts represented in the content. By building from what students already know about the content, you can easily move into a discussion about what more they would like to learn about the content. Use this as a tool to expand students' understanding of the content and their level of curiosity, using images such as those that make up the Civil War Photo Collage illustrated in figure 4.2.

Engage students with the content. Some students may be surprised to find out that there were naval battles during the Civil War. Seeing images of the events, locations, and armaments from the Civil War may engage students and serve to help them develop the skills to become independent, lifelong learners, able to build on their natural curiosity.

**Figure 5.2. Civil War Photo Collage. Author created. Photo source: Library of Congress**

*ABC Brainstorm*

The ABC Brainstorm is a fun and quick assessment. Simply provide students with a sheet of paper with the alphabet listed down the lefthand margin. Have the students write a word that relates to the unit of study for each letter of the alphabet. For example, if the class were studying the weather you might write: A—April, B—barometer, and so on. Then you could have students write a summary paragraph about the topic of weather, using, in part, the vocabulary list they've created with their alphabet list. "April relates to barometer because in April the barometer goes up and it begins to rain (or snow, as the case may be)."

This is a quick and easy way to evaluate students' knowledge of the vocabulary associated with the content. The complexity of the responses can help you identify the level of the students' understanding. Do they use scientifically correct terms like *barometer* or *precipitation* or more common vocabulary such as *hot* or *rain*? Additionally, the vocabulary list serves as a useful prompt to support students as they write about the content. Their ability to accurately use the vocabulary will help you identify the level, breadth, and depth of their understanding of the content.

The ability to generate a list of vocabulary words is far different from the ability to use that vocabulary correctly and accurately in writing. You can use the information gleaned from this assessment not only to teach vocabulary skills but also to build students' skill in using content-specific terminology to describe, for example, weather phenomena. As always, be aware of the varied levels and consider differentiating instruction based upon students' vocabulary and their ability to use this vocabulary accurately.

*Interviews*

Brief but structured interviews with randomly selected individuals or groups of students will allow us to evaluate the extent to which students are learning the concepts and skills we are working to teach. To be efficient and usable, these interviews must necessarily be brief. Therefore the questions asked need to be carefully selected and be directly related to the content of concern. They could consist of a series of tasks or problems or questions that require students to synthesize information already taught. For example, in a government class you might ask, "Given the upcoming election, what issues do you consider to be the most important?"

Again, we need to record this data, identifying the level of knowledge and understanding the students demonstrate during the interview. Do they have a strong understanding of the current political issues? How broad is their view? Do they have a community, state, national, or world focus? The responses need to be categorized, identifying levels of knowledge demonstrated by the students being interviewed.

We need to identify what topics the students know well and what topics seem to be consistently weak for those students being interviewed. Are there differences? Are there some learners who have a broad but thin understanding of the content, who are able to discuss the political process but are unable to discuss the current election, or who have a narrow but deep understanding, focusing on one issue without any awareness of other political issues of current importance? This information should be used to develop learning activities to address varying learning needs, engaging students in current political issues or helping students identify other issues that are not currently being addressed and writing their own legislative agenda.

If you choose to interview every student, you can use this information to group specific students according to the data obtained. The key to being successful when using this with every student is in developing an easy system for tracking the individual student's skill and knowledge. A simple checklist or log can be used to document the student's performance in each portion of the interview.

## IMPLEMENTATION

Preassessments that address learner characteristics should be completed early in the school year. Data should be recorded on an information sheet for each student. In the younger grades, you can laminate each and stick them to the student's desk, or use contact paper or clear packing tape to tape them to the student's desk. This will allow you, as you move around the room, to provide students with support based upon their individual learning characteristics. Some teachers use visual icons that help them quickly identify the students' learning preferences without allowing other students to stereotype one another and use it as a weapon against one another.

At the beginning of the semester or school year, also assess students' prior knowledge as it relates to prerequisites and foundational skills that need to be in place in order for students to learn the content being addressed. Take the time to develop supports or reteach specific key concepts or skills that will help the students be successful in your class. Prior

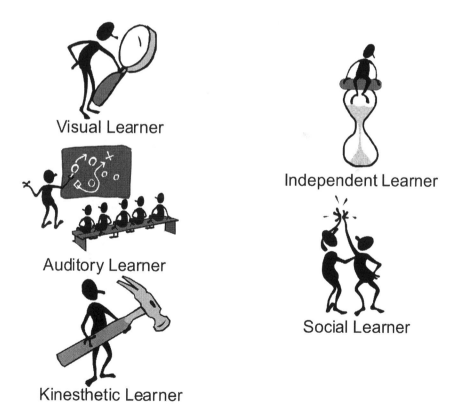

**Figure 5.3. Possible Learning Style Icons**

to the beginning of each unit, preassess your students on the upcoming unit and use this information to design instruction and to group students during the unit. Preassessments should be short and easy to quickly score and record data for future use.

Ideally, evaluate student performance on preassessments holistically. A simple rubric that evaluates responses on the degree of detail the student is able to provide is ideal. When differentiating instruction for students, it works well to be able to identify three levels of learners:

1. Learners who have already learned the content to be addressed with a strong understanding
2. Learners who are at grade level and are prepared to learn the new content
3. Learners who are below grade level with limited preparation and foundational knowledge related to the concepts to be taught

You might think that the same students will make up each group for every unit, and this may be true but is seldom always true. Evaluating student preparation and current knowledge of the content at the beginning of each unit will allow you to flexibly group students and provide instruction at the level and in a style most appropriate for their learning needs.

## CONCLUSION

Don't feel that you have to do everything. Select! We need to take the time to determine what is most important and relevant to us and our students. The data available from conducting preassessments can be a powerful tool if it is used to inform instruction, helping you maximize learning time and develop differentiated instruction. Based on the findings, teachers can develop multiple pathways to address learning goals.

Before a unit of instruction begins, learning tasks can be designed that best meet students' individual needs as well as the collective needs of the entire class. By anticipating student needs, you will be able to avoid losing students either because of lack of skill or boredom. You will know the students who need extra support as well as those who need an opportunity to move ahead and work with the content at a different level.

To be effective, preassessments need to be closely tied to the intended learning outcomes of a unit. In creating the preassessment, attend to the foundational knowledge and skills that will be necessary for students to succeed as well as the content to be addressed. In analyzing the results of the preassessment, maintain that level of clarity. What information does the assessment provide you as it relates to the learning outcomes identified? This clarity is essential to obtaining useful, reliable, and valid information in terms of student learning and its application to the content.

Just as with any assessment, make sure that there is alignment between the learning outcome and the assessment instrument. If your goal is for students to analyze a given set of data and make suggestions as to how to proceed, it will not work to administer a multiple choice assessment. Utilize preassessments that closely align with how you want the students to be able to use what they learn.

Finally, keep the assessment concise and efficient. This will allow you to maintain a high level of interest for the students, not boring them with the assessment. It will also maximize your instructional time, allowing you to quickly analyze the information gleaned and in turn implement it in your instruction. If you try to capture too much information, this will work against you, becoming too time consuming for you and your students to be provide valuable information.

# SIX

# Commercial Short-Cycle Assessments

From Response to Intervention (RTI) (identified as a method for dealing with learning disabilities in the 2004 reauthorization of the Individuals with Disabilities Act) and other associated practices used to respond to student academic needs, an entire commercial industry focused on formative assessment has grown. In the industry these formative assessments are more frequently referred to as "short-cycle assessments." These assessments are designed to be administered three to four times per year, at minimum, and they provide diagnostic information related to specific content standards.

In this chapter we will review briefly the RTI process and look at a number of commercially available short-cycle assessment systems that can be used to support the formative assessment process. The assessments include tools that are used to assess basic reading skills, as well as content knowledge in English, math, science, and, in a few cases, social studies. We will look specifically at DIBELS, Texas Primary Reading Inventory, STAR Assessments, Measured Progress, MAP, Edmentum, and The Developing Reading Assessment.

## RESPONSE TO INTERVENTION (RTI)

In the last few years formative assessment has taken a forefront position, as educators have taken a strong look at the need to track student progress. Formative assessment moved into a forward role when special education research focused on the identification and classification of students with learning disabilities. Through research it was noted that learning disabilities are not the result of medical or social conditions that can impede learning. Instead they are diagnoses that are made based upon what the students are not, rather than what they are (Lyon et al. 2001).

The variety of conditions and environmental constraints that can result in learning difficulties led to the development of an intervention system designed to be applied in the general education classroom. Implementing a system prior to identifying students as special needs learners allows the needs of all students to be addressed. The tiered system utilized in response to intervention allows for varying levels of support and resources to be implemented based upon a student's needs as identified through the use of short-cycle assessments. Thus interventions can be implemented for students with minor difficulties before they grow to become major difficulties.

For example, students who miss school when a key concept is being taught may be challenged by this lack of knowledge throughout their school career. If a student misses school while learning the multiplication tables, for instance, the student will have difficulty developing other math skills involving multiplication as he or she progresses in school. A student who is reading below grade level will have difficulty as well. By implementing a tiered system, the teacher can address the needs of each child through an instructional intervention, before the learning difficulty becomes a learning disability and requires special education services.

Born from special education research and the desire to address the instructional needs of learning disabled (LD) students, the RTI process has become a mandate used to support the learning of all students. A three-tier process has been defined for use in meeting student needs and eventually identifying those students with special needs. Formative assessment plays a key role in this process. In the RTI process, formative assessment is used to identify students who are not mastering the identified learning goals.

At Tier 1, all students receive whole group instruction founded in research-based instructional strategies designed to support learning. Differentiated instruction is highly supported in this process. At Tier 2, students who are not responding well to whole group instructional strategies receive extended instruction in small groups. If a student is still not achieving at an appropriate level, he or she is taken to Tier 3 and receives extended instruction individually.

The focus is on differentiating instruction and implementing research-based interventions matched to individual student need. Throughout the process, formative assessment is used to monitor student progress during the instruction interventions, to determine if students are meeting the defined learning goals (Klotz 2007).

With the increased focus on formative assessment in the classroom and the use of data to inform instruction, commercial products have become increasingly available. The overwhelming majority of these products are computer-based. They are typically designed to adjust to the students' capabilities. If a student answers a question correctly, the next question is harder. If the question is answered incorrectly, the following question is easier. The questions are leveled, allowing the computer to identify the level at which the student is performing.

A well-written assessment that is designed to assess performance on a specific standard down to the individual indicator can provide detailed information as to a student's mastery of a specific skill or concept. Although purchase of a short-cycle assessment system can be expensive, if the system is used to track student progress and the data are used to support student learning, over an extended period of time, commercial assessments can be a cost-effective and efficient means of tracking student learning.

## DYNAMIC INDICATORS OF BASIC EARLY LITERACY SKILLS (DIBELS)

The Dynamic Indicators of Basic Early Literacy Skills (DIBELS) and literacy assessments for native Spanish speakers called IDEL (Indicadores Dinámicos del Éxito en la Lectura) (University of Oregon Center on Teaching and Learning 2007a) are a collection of reading assessments designed to monitor reading progress of students in grades pre-K through 6. The purpose of the assessments is to identify students who need additional support and instruction. DIBELS includes a database designed to track student progress and collate data for school and district reports. Reports can be generated immediately to provide feedback designed to support instructional decisions.

Assessments included in DIBELS focus on the foundational skills of reading and phonemic awareness, and they were developed to be used by teachers to regularly monitor the development of prereading and early reading skills (University of Oregon Center on Teaching and Learning 2007b). Individual measures are used to assess students' phonemic awareness, phonics, reading fluency, vocabulary, and reading comprehension. These have been identified as critical skills necessary for successful readers.

Each assessment is conducted one-on-one with each child and takes about one minute to complete; on average an entire assessment takes less than ten minutes to complete, depending on grade level and time of year. Benchmark assessments are given three times during the academic year: fall, winter, and spring. Teachers may also choose to give the assessment at other times to monitor the progress of students who need extra reading support. The assessments are designed to be indicators of overall reading status, not a comprehensive assessment of reading ability. As a formative assessment, this is ideal because it allows the teacher to obtain valuable data without taking up large amounts of instructional time.

Reports can be generated for collated groups of students as well as individual students. Individual student reports compare the student's actual performance to the level at which students are expected to perform at the given point in the school year. Reports show student performance not only for the current school year but also for previous grade levels. Given these reports, teachers can easily use the data to identify literacy skills that they need to focus on for the entire class as well as for individual students.

## TEXAS PRIMARY READING INVENTORY (TPRI)

The Texas Primary Reading Inventory (TPRI) and the Tejas Lee (Texas Institute for Measurement, Evaluation, and Statistics 2010), an early reading assessment for native Spanish speakers, are both designed to assess the reading development of students in grades K through 3. The assessment measures phonemic awareness, graphophonemic knowledge, reading accuracy, fluency, and comprehension. There are two sections to the assessment: a screening section, which is a brief measure designed to predict which students may need additional or intensive reading support, and an inventory section, which is a diagnostic tool to identify specific strengths and challenges for each student.

TPRI is a branching assessment that depends on the student's performance and grade level to determine which sections should be given to the student. Because of this, the time it takes to give the assessment can vary. On average it takes about twenty minutes per student to deliver the one-on-one assessment. The assessment is designed to be delivered three times per year: fall, winter, and spring. Teachers record assessment results for each student in a summary sheet that is provided with the assessment. The summary sheet is an Excel file designed to provide teachers with an overview of the results based on their data entry. The results are designed to be used by teachers to better plan instruction for individual students.

## STAR ASSESSMENTS

Renaissance Learning (2013) provides three short-cycle monitoring assessments designed to assess student learning in early literacy, reading, and mathematics, for students in grades K through 12. The assessments are aligned with state standards and the Common Core State Standards (CCSS).

These computer-based assessments make use of computer-adaptive testing and item response theory to allow for efficient, individualized assessment of student learning. Depending on the student's response to a question, the computer adjusts with the next question, giving a question that is either more or less difficult. The system is designed to adapt based on the student's performance and to measure student growth. Assessments take fifteen to twenty minutes to complete and are expected to be given three times per year: fall, winter, and spring.

The system provides reports that can be used for screening, progress monitoring, instructional planning, and to determine student performance in relation to state standards and the Common Core State Standards. The company also provides supplemental materials to help teachers support instruction based upon assessment findings. The system charts a learning path for each student, providing instructional resources to address the identified learning needs. Tools are provided for teachers to use in identifying prerequisite skills, developing critical thinking skills, and planning the steps to be taken to meet the standards.

## MEASURED PROGRESS

Measured Progress (Foundation/Progressive Policy Institute 2013) sells an assessment tool called DATAWISE™. This is an assessment and data management tool designed to support the formative assessment process. This tool can be used by teachers to develop their own computer-based assessments, or they can use an item bank designed to assess the Common Core State Standards. This system can support the development of a large item bank of questions that can be used across the district by all teachers.

You can choose to use teacher-created items or items from the Measured Progress item bank to develop classroom, school, or district assessments. You can also choose to use a program extension called FIXED FORMS™. These are prebuilt assessments that are designed to assess student growth in English language arts and mathematics for grades 3 to 11.

Assessments can be administered online or they can be printed out and administered using paper and pencil. You can print Quick Test bubble sheets or use test booklets in collecting student responses. These can both be easily scanned and scored by the system and imported into DATAWISE™.

You can also use Student Response Devices to collect student data during instruction. These devices look similar to remote controls. During your lesson you can include questions. Students respond by keying in a response to each question on their individual device. The system scores and collates student responses and provides the teacher with immediate feedback regarding student performance. This tool can be used to adjust instruction on the fly, right as you are delivering the lesson.

Data using the FIXED FORMS™ assessments are reported with scaled scores and performance level descriptors. This tool allows teachers to track student growth from year to year, using Lexile® and Quantile® scores. With this system, you can generate a Student Profile report, which provides an overview of student performance over multiple years for individual students or a group of students.

You can also generate a Student Progress report, which compares student performance on two tests, or a Proficiency Over Standards report, which shows the performance of individual students on a standard by using the results of one or more tests. Each of these can be used to support the formative assessment process and the design of instruction to address individual and group learning needs.

## NORTHWEST EVALUATION ASSOCIATION'S MEASURES OF ACADEMIC PROGRESS® (MAP®)

The Northwest Evaluation Association's (NWEA) Measures of Academic Progress® (MAP®) (2013) is a computer-based adaptive assessment system that adjusts the difficulty of questions up or down based upon the student's performance. These are short-cycle assessments that can be used to measure and monitor student growth in math, science, English, and reading. The measures are designed for use in grades K through 12 and are aligned to national and state curricula.

MAP tests are administered up to four times a year through an online system. This allows teachers to closely monitor the progress of students. Student test results are maintained and stored annually, so teachers and parents can monitor the growth of individual students year after year. Scores are reported based on item difficulty and student performance.

Because item difficulty is reported on the RIT scale (for Rasch unIT) with an equal interval between each level of difficulty, student progress can be tracked over time. Reference charts allow teachers to examine student performance on individual standards and performance indicators. These data allow teachers to track student growth and mastery of specific topics.

With access to aggregated student reports, building and central office administrators can use MAP data to inform curriculum and school improvement decisions. Educators can use MAP tests to identify the skills and concepts individual students have learned; diagnose instructional needs of individual students; monitor academic growth over time; make data-driven decisions at the classroom, school, and district levels; and help place new students into appropriate instructional programs.

## EDMENTUM

Edmentum Assessments (2012) provides a suite of assessment tools that range from diagnostic assessments to formative assessments that can be used to support student learning and monitor student progress. Assessments are available for reading, writing, and mathematics. In addition to assessing student performance, the system provides support to the teacher by prescribing content that can be used to address learning gaps identified through the assessment process.

## DEVELOPMENTAL READING ASSESSMENT (DRA)

The Developmental Reading Assessment (Scholastic 2013) focuses on foundational reading skills, much the same as DIBELS does. This benchmarking assessment was originally developed by a group of educators to assess students' reading level.

The test is administered individually, with the student reading a benchmark book to the teacher and then retelling the story. Tasks are divided into three skill sets: phonemic awareness, the alphabetic principle/phonics, and fluency. The student is scored on accuracy of reading, comprehension, and fluency. The identified reading level is then used to help students select books that are appropriate for their reading skills. This assessment is traditionally administered on an annual or semiannual basis.

Pearson (2013) has developed an assessment tool to be used by educators in administering a Developmental Reading Assessment. This system provides the teacher with an electronic tool that can be used to score the assessment. The system analyzes the assessment data collected and provides individual and class results that graphically represent student performance. Data can be stored, allowing for longitudinal monitoring of student performance. The system can also generate a class profile that can be used to help group students based on specific learning needs.

## ACHIEVE

Achieve (Achieve n.d.) is a program that was originally designed to predict how students would score on standardized assessments. It is a multiple choice assessment that can be used to monitor student progress in reading, language arts, mathematics, science, and social studies for grades 1 through 12.

The tests are normally administered three times per year: fall, winter, and spring. All three exams can be administered as paper-and-pencil assessments, or two of the assessments may be administered online and the final assessment administered using paper and pencil. To administer the assessment, the company sends a packet to schools with instructions, answer sheets, and test booklets. It is very much a traditional standards-based assessment tool. Those tests administered offline are mailed to Achieve and the company returns color-coded reports within seven to ten days.

Reports returned to the school include a schoolwide report that reports overall school performance on benchmarks. Similar reports are also provided for each grade, each individual class, and each student. A separate benchmark report provides performance data for every question associated with a specific benchmark. With the second and third assessments, a schoolwide comparison report and a report that compares classes are available. A report designed for parents is also available online. The company suggests using these reports during parent-teacher conferences.

## CONCLUSION

As demonstrated in this chapter, there are a number of commercial short-cycle assessments that are designed to support the formative assessment process. In this chapter, a basic overview of some of the more prominent assessments has been provided. Descriptions have been provided for multiple assessments designed to measure student progress at multiple points during the academic year. Tests range from paper-and-pencil assessments that are either scanned into a computer for analysis or sent to the company, which then provides analysis, to more sophisticated systems that can be completed entirely online.

Assessments that adapt to the difficulty of the questions asked based upon student responses seem to provide the best analysis of student performance. Commercial, short-cycle assessments provide us with information that we may use to better address student learning needs. The more immediately the analysis of student performance is available, the more likely the data will be able to be used to inform instruction. It should be noted, however, that while commercial, short-cycle assessments are an efficient method for gathering formative assessment data, they are meant to meet the needs of a broad audience. They may not be directly related to the learning needs of your classroom.

# SEVEN

## Collaborative Learning

Many students and teachers do not like collaborative learning projects. They are concerned over the lack of individual input by students into the final product. There is a reasonable fear that one student will end up doing all of the work while others coast. In a poorly designed activity, it is easy for some students to sit back and let one or two of their teammates do all the work. Individual as well as group accountability is key to dealing with this situation. It is also important to understand the difference between cooperative and collaborative learning.

When you cooperate, the members of the team agree to support a decision. They may not have helped come up with the decision. They may not even agree with the decision. But they have agreed to support the decision. Collaborative learning requires input and agreement from all team members. It is a shared decision and a product that requires input from and support by all team members. The very nature of collaboration reinforces the importance of individual accountability as well as group accountability.

If a collaborative activity is well designed, the input of all team members will be necessary to the successful completion of the learning activity. Simply stating that individual participation and input is required in the directions for the activity is not sufficient. The requirement for individual input and accountability must be evident in the activity itself.

An activity requiring students to complete a set of worksheets together is not an activity that requires collaboration. A group of three students could simply split up the worksheets, each taking responsibility for one. They could simply make three copies of the same worksheet, and the activity would be done—no collaboration needed.

A well-designed collaborative learning activity is one in which the product will be better because of the collaboration. It is one that requires the individual skills and abilities of each team member to come together to create a product that is better than they could develop singly. It is one that is authentic and resembles to many extents a project that would be completed in the real world. There are not too many jobs in the world today that require employees to work in total isolation. To be productive and efficient and to move the job forward, collaboration is essential. This is how collaborative learning activities should be in the classroom as well.

We can also make use of collaborative, pair-and-share activities to track student understanding. Activities such as a structured review, in which students work with partners to share what they've learned, can also be effective. In this chapter we will explore the use of collaborative learning activities to support the formative assessment process, examining the design of collaborative learning activities to foster individual as well as group accountability.

## STRUCTURE OF THE COLLABORATIVE ACTIVITY TO SUPPORT USE AS FORMATIVE ASSESSMENT

In designing a collaborative activity that can serve as a formative assessment, four key constructs need to be in place. First, to work as a formative assessment, the collaborative learning activity needs to be structured so as to allow the teacher to track individual as well as group performance. Second, the activity needs to be designed so that a single individual could not perform the activity alone. Group input should be required to complete the activity or project. Third, in forming groups, individual skills and qualities each team member will bring to the group should be considered.

Design activities that require the specific skills and abilities each team member brings to the team. It is not always possible to build activities that incorporate every individual skill brought to the table. It is, however, important to acknowledge, support, and utilize the individual skills, abilities, and even interests that each student brings to the class.

Finally, just as ideally happens in the work world, teams are formed to take advantage of the specific skills and abilities that each individual will bring to the team. It is important that this be done in the classroom as well. Groups need to be more than a random selection of students. At times teams need to be formed strategically. When teams are strategically organized based on individual skills and abilities, each student is allowed to become a valued part of the team. Each student is able to contribute to the team, rather than being a leech who merely takes advantage of the other members of the team.

## ACCOUNTABILITY

As mentioned previously, individual as well as group accountability must be in place. The final project will be assessed for group performance, but individual input into that final project should also be assessed. There are a variety of means to track individual participation. One of the simplest is to ask students to evaluate their participation and input as well as that of their teammates through a simple survey. A Likert scale survey that asks the students to rate individual participation of each team member is easiest. Open-ended questions that ask team members about individual contributions are also appropriate.

For example, a survey could be set up and might include the following questions for each team member: What percentage of the project did [team member's name] complete? What specific things did [team member's name] bring to the project? Would you like to work with this team member again? Why or why not? What special skills did this team member bring to this project? For the first question, include options based upon the number of students on each team. For example, if the students were organized into teams of four, the options might be (a) 25%, (b) 50%, (c) 75%, (d) 100%, and (e) did not participate to any significant extent.

Other methods of tracking individual participation include developing check-in sheets that are used at varying points during the progression of a project. Students log what they are working on at each point and what information or tasks are their responsibility. Depending on the developmental level of the students, this can be completed independently by the student and monitored by the teacher, or it may be done collaboratively through individual meetings between the teacher and the student.

## COLLABORATIVE LEARNING ACTIVITIES

As you consider how you will implement collaborative learning into your classroom, consider what it is that you want the students to learn. While some view collaboration as a means to an end, collaboration in and of itself can be an important part of what is to be learned as well as the learning process. "In some collaborative activities, collaboration is focused on producing a group project, in others it is designed to improve the quality of individual work" and learning (Swan, Shen, and Hiltz 2006).

As we look at using collaborative activities for formative assessment, we will focus on activities designed to improve student learning. In the following section, directions will be provided for specific collaborative learning activities that lend themselves easily to the formative assessment process, including pair and share, Student Teams Achievement Divisions, structured review, and so on.

*Think, Pair, Share*

A think, pair, share activity is a good place to begin. This is an activity that can be accomplished quickly, with a limited amount of frustration on the part of the teacher and the students. It is a good way to start the basics of teaching collaboration and monitoring individual understanding of the learning outcomes. This activity provides time and structure for students to think about a given topic or question.

Prior to the learning activity, students are grouped into teams of two or, at the most, three students. During instruction a question, situation, or topic is posed to the students, and they are given time to think and formulate individual ideas about the issue. They then share their ideas with their team. The students discuss their ideas, expanding on their individual responses and increasing their level of engagement. After a specified period of time, pairs then share the outcome of their discussion with the rest of the class.

For example, a math class may be working on word problems, applying various formulas they have been studying. Students are given a word problem that includes not only relevant information, but also unnecessary data designed to distract them. They need to determine the relevant facts needed to solve the problem and select the appropriate formula(s).

In implementing this exercise as a think, pair, share activity, students would first identify individually what they thought were the relevant data and formula(s) to use in solving the problem. They would then discuss with their partner(s) the data in the word problem. They would identify together the relevant data and determine the formula(s) to be used to solve the problem. The class would then share out their findings and work to solve the problem. Teams could work on the same problem, or each team could work on a different problem, explaining to their classmates how they selected the appropriate data and formula(s) they used to solve the problem.

To use this as an assessment tool, the teacher would need to track the responses of individual teams. During the discussion, the teacher can circulate and listen to the individual comments, noting student performance, areas of concern, and strong points on a log sheet. This information can be utilized during the current lesson to reinforce specific learning outcomes, or it can be used at a later date to revise or enhance further instruction.

In your observations, you will need to focus on the information that will help you document student learning relevant to the learning outcomes you are wanting to assess. In the example provided, it would be important to pay attention to which pairs of students were able to differeniate between relevant and irrelevant information and determine the relevant data and formula(s).

*Numbered Heads Together*

Similar to pair and share, groups of three or four students work together to derive an answer to a problem presented to them. In this activity students are counted off into groups. Ideally there would be no more than five students in each group. Each group would, preferably, be made up of an equal number of students, ideally three or four students. The membership of each group would also have a heterogeneous mix of learning abilities, with teams approximately equal in the range of abilities represented. Within each team, each student is assigned a number.

Once the groups are arranged, a question is posed to the class as a whole. Questions should have a limited number of correct responses. These questions need to be clear, knowledge level questions or questions that ask the students to describe a clear process. For example, "How do you find the square root of a number?" or "What are the four main characteristics of a reptile?" After the question is posed, give the students a specified amount of time, one to three minutes, to come together and talk quietly about the question.

The team determines the correct answer by bringing their heads together and consulting with one another. Once the correct answer has been identified, the team is responsible for making sure that every student on the team knows the correct answer. The team will earn a point only if the student whose number is called knows the correct answer.

When time is up, select a random number between 1 and 4 and have the student on each team with that number stand. At this point, you may randomly select a team to respond (making sure that during the course of the game each team gets an equal number of opportunities to respond) or you can have each representative write down his or her response on a small whiteboard, a piece of paper, or a chalkboard. In this case, the team would receive a point for each representative with the correct response.

This exercise works well as a review activity. It gives you an opportunity to not only review the content with students, but also to reinforce learning by helping those students who have not mastered the content learn information they had formerly missed. In using this as a formative assessment, questions need to align closely with the learning outcomes selected for evaluation.

During the activity itself, you will need to monitor individual as well as group performance. While attending to individual performance, the teacher would need to observe and note which students were actively participating, making specific note of misconceptions or misunderstandings during group work. The responses of the various teams would also need to be tracked, noting the performace of each team and the concepts or constructs with which students had difficulty.

*Structured Review*

The structured review is typically done as a think, pair, share activity. Pairs of students are given a series of questions to discuss or an activity to complete. Progressively, each question or activity becomes more narrow and defined (Dirksen 2011). For example, in an English class students may be asked to define the terms *theme, setting,* and *protagonist*. Next, the students could be asked to identify these same things for a series of short reading selections. Finally, the students would identify these same things for a book such as *Treasure Island*.

Traditionally, students are given forty seconds to discuss the first question, thirty seconds for the second, twenty seconds for the third, and ten seconds for the last one. As you can tell from my example, the time frame may vary, but the intent is the same. The discussion is gradually focused and narrowed, and the students' understanding is revealed and clarified.

When using this type of activity to gather formative assessment data, the teacher needs to actively monitor student work. Each group should be provided with a worksheet on which to record their responses. To gather individual performance data, the teacher should circulate around the room, noting observational data on a tracking sheet. On the tracking sheet, space should be provided to record individual performance for each identified learning objective.

A simple, three-point rubric can be used to describe each student's performance, and observational data should be recorded regarding areas of concern. Misconceptions identified during the learning activity should be dealt with immediately, and opportunities for reteaching certain concepts should be planned.

*Jigsaw*

In a jigsaw activity students are assigned to two teams: an expert team and a teaching team. In the expert team, students work with their team members to develop expertise in a specific concept or construct. Once they have developed their expertise, students then move from the expert team to separate teaching teams. Each team member on the teaching team has developed expertise with a different concept or construct.

In the teaching team, students teach their team members what they learned while working in their expert team. Each member shares the knowledge gained in the expert team, teaching their new team what he or she learned. Together, each member of the teaching team works to help the other members of the new team master the content they have brought from their expert team.

In a social studies class, expert teams may be organized to study different types of governance: democracy, socialism, anarchy, capitalism, communism, and the like. Each team would study their assigned topic. Then a member from each expert team would come together with other students from other expert teams to form a teaching team. They would each teach their group about the topic in which they had developed expertise. So if you had four expert teams, each with five members, you would end up with five teaching teams, each with four members.

By monitoring the expert teams as well as the teaching teams, the teacher can check the students' understanding and knowledge of the content. Student activity in both the expert teams and teaching teams needs to be monitored closely to ensure that the students are not learning and teaching misconceptions, which would lead to greater learning issues. In checking the expert team's progress, the teacher can check their thinking and understanding to determine if they are on the right track. In monitoring the teaching teams, the teacher can help clarify points and help the experts further develop their own understanding of the concepts being taught.

Again, individual student progress can be monitored using a tracking sheet that is associated with a simple rubric. Student performance as it relates to each learning outcome should be monitored and comments recorded regarding specific performance issues.

### Student Teams Achievement Divisions

Teams are organized heterogeneously for Student Teams Achievement Divisions. Teams are organized so that there is a good mix of ability levels. Each team should be made up of high-, low-, and middle-ability students. In this activity, students work together to improve the performance of each team member. A preassessment related to the identified learning outcomes is given to the class as a whole. Student performance on this preassessment serves as a baseline measure to determine student gains. The baseline scores for each team member of each group should be recorded.

After the activity is completed, a postassessment will be given. These scores will also be recorded. The preassessment score will be subtracted from the postassessment score to determine a gain score for each student. The team's overall score is based on the sum of the gain scores recorded for each team member. The team with the highest gain score is determined to be the winner.

After the preassessment, students work on learning activities and projects identified by the teacher, working to develop mastery of the objectives by all of the students. To win, it is essential that the team members work together to help all the students on the team develop their individual skills and abilities. Learning activities might include problem-solving activities, games, group discussion, role play, and so on.

This is a learning activity that really brings to life the idea that learning can be a collaborative endeavor and should work as any other team activity. In basketball or any other team sport, the success of the team is determined by their ability to work together. With Student Teams Achievement Divisions, it is the same. The team must work together to achieve.

The team will gain the most when the lower-level students achieve at higher levels. The scores obtained by the lower-ability students typically have the greater room for improvement. But these students have to be engaged in the learning; without collaborative work their scores won't improve as dramatically as they could. By the same token, advanced students will be able to increase their own understanding of the content by helping those with less skill develop their own understanding.

In using Standard Teams Achievement Division as a formative assessment tool, the teacher must keep close track of individual team performance on the learning activities. Active participation is essential to the success of this collaborative activity. Assessment data gained from the preassessment and postassessment can be used to identify areas in which students need more instruction and support. By tracking student and group progress throughout the learning process, you can also supplement the activities as deemed necessary. You can use the observational data to improve student performance during the activity, and not just after the postassessment.

## IMPLEMENTATION

Collaborative learning activities can be engaging, effective learning tools that can be used to support formative assessment if the data is tracked and utilized. To be effective and engaging, the activities need to be designed so that student participation is maximized.

Once students are engaged and involved, individual performance on group projects should be monitored closely, with the intent of helping students develop their collaborative skills as well as content knowledge. Active observation of group work by the teacher can help identify where students not only need additional content instruction but also instruction on social and collaborative work skills.

In addition to structuring the activity so that individual accountability and participation is enhanced, assessment tools need to be designed to address individual as well as group learning. As we look at the use of collaborative learning to support the formative assessment process, this is especially important. Logs on which teams or individual students can record their answers or document group work need to be developed for some of the collaborative activities.

To track individual performance on the identified learning outcomes, a tracking sheet should be developed. This tracking sheet should be used to document students' performance and record comments related to their performance. To make it easier to quickly record an evaluation of student performance, develop a simple, three-point rubric that clearly describes three levels of performance. For example, you might define mastery, developing, and intervention needed. On the tracking sheet, create columns for student names and each learning outcome to be assessed. Provide space to record a numerical score, and additional space to record specific comments that can be used to guide future instruction.

Classroom management is key to the successful implementation of collaborative learning. The teacher must be an active presence in the classroom, monitoring student progress and engaging students who are not actively participating. Students need to understand your expectations during cooperative learning activities. Specific consequences and rewards need to be in place to reinforce your expectations. It is important that you actively monitor student participation and student behavior and respond to inappropriate conduct immediately.

Consistency is essential. If students know that you will not require them to meet your expectations at all times, they will not meet those expectations. While collaborative learning can engage students and reduce classroom management issues, it is also an opportunity for students to become off-task and let others do the work. To be effective, the entire class has to be acting as a team when participating in collaborative learning, supporting the learning of all students with every student actively engaged.

## CONCLUSION

Collaborative learning is a powerful instructional tool and can also be used to effectively and efficiently support the formative assessment process. To be used effectively, engaging activities need to be developed that require the participation of all students to successfully complete the activity. Activities need to be relevant and engaging to the students. The learning environment needs to be supportive of team work, with students working together to help all students master the content.

Assessment tools such as log sheets, tracking sheets, and simplified rubrics need to be developed so that the teacher can quickly and efficiently record data regarding student achievement and team performance. Observational data should also be recorded, which identifies concepts that may need to be reinforced or retaught.

Misconceptions need to be addressed immediately, during group learning, to avoid the spread of misinformation. In this chapter we explored a number of collaborative learning activities that can be used specifically to support the formative assessment process. Each of these learning activities can be used to not only foster student learning but also to gather data relative to student performance that can be used to inform instructional decisions.

# EIGHT
## Writing

Writing is one aspect of the curriculum that is mirrored across all content areas. "Writing across the curriculum" has been a popular mantra for the last several decades. Most teachers have implemented some form of writing into their classes. The need for students to be able to express themselves effectively in all content areas provides teachers with the opportunity to use student writing as part of their formative assessment process. Additionally, as you engage your students in writing about what they are learning, you will help them reinforce and build their understanding of the content. In this chapter we will explore the use of specific writing activities across the curriculum to inform the formative assessment process.

Writing provides us a tool with which students can demonstrate the depth and breadth of their content knowledge. When used as a tool for formative assessment, writing assignments should be part of the standard operating procedure for the classroom. Writing should not be an occasional, on-again-off-again activity. Students need to be comfortable with the tools we use to assess their learning. If writing is to be used as an effective assessment tool, students need to be comfortable with writing as part of their learning.

Writing prompts need to encourage an in-depth focus on specific learning objectives, as well as allowing for breadth in the students' responses. The validity of the students' written response will be enhanced if they view their writing as being important. They need to be writing for more than a grade and the teacher's red pen. Whenever possible, provide students with writing opportunities that give them another audience. "Students' motivation and commitment levels will be much higher if they know that their writing is going to have an impact on someone else and will not simply be the source of a grade" (Peterson 2007, 32).

The writing strategies discussed in this chapter focus on casual writing. This type of writing is designed to serve as a building block for more complex thinking and learning. Casual writing is designed to be supportive of future learning, rather than as an end in itself (Peha 2003).

So that casual writing can be used reliably as an assessment tool, we need to model for students our expectations regarding their writing. We also need to help students overcome their anxieties about writing. Students need to feel comfortable when writing about their ideas and thinking. By modeling casual writing, we can foster this comfort. This can be further supported by taking time to teach students how to organize their writing so that the product will be useful to us as a formative assessment measure and also useful to them so that they can use what they have learned later.

## WRITING ACTIVITIES

Writing activities, especially casual writing activities, can be easily integrated into most curricula. Writing helps our students think more deeply about the content and about their own thinking about the concepts they are learning. It also engages students with higher levels of thinking and reasoning (Brozo and Simpson 2003). Writing can also lead to greater understanding of concepts across the curriculum, requiring students to sort through and organize information and make sense of ideas (Peterson 2007).

Casual writing, such as free-writes and journal writing, makes a good tool to assess students' knowledge of the content. It can allow us to "sit beside" our students and see how their minds work (Peha 2003). In the following section we look at a number of writing activities that can be easily utilized as formative assessments, including quick writes, weekly summaries, timed or free writes, ticket out, journaling, and ACE.

### Quick Write / Quick Draw

A Quick Write / Quick Draw activity makes use of visual skills. Folding a sheet of paper in half or using two or more sheets of paper, students write about and draw a concept, writing on one half of the paper and drawing on the other half. They can begin with either drawing or writing, whichever they prefer. For example, you might have them complete a Quick Write / Quick Draw on the human circulatory system.

Doing both a written and drawn explanation will help them make better sense of the concept, and it will give you a clear picture of what they know and the depth and breadth of their knowledge. This also allows you to tap into multiple learning and thinking styles. Students may be able to demonstrate their knowledge better through drawing and art

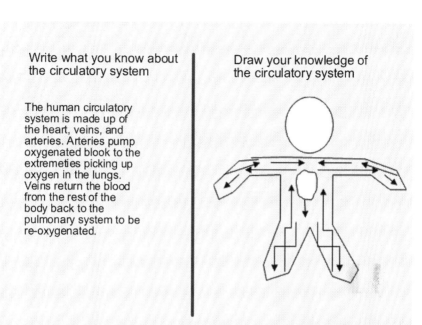

Write what you know about the circulatory system

The human circulatory system is made up of the heart, veins, and arteries. Arteries pump oxygenated blook to the extremeties picking up oxygen in the lungs. Veins return the blood from the rest of the body back to the pulmonary system to be re-oxygenated.

Draw your knowledge of the circulatory system

**Figure 8.1.   Quick Write_Draw on the Circulatory System**

than through the written word, or vice versa. The students' understanding of the content as well as their preferred learning styles and ability to write can be assessed using this preassessment.

It's key here to look for inconsistencies between the written and visual descriptions. Can a student provide a visual representation of the circulatory system (see figure 8.1) but not a written description? Does he or she have a clear understanding of the circulatory system, but is unable to describe it in writing?

As an addition to this assessment, consider including oral descriptions. By looking beyond a student's written explanation, you will be able to identify learners who understand the content but are unable to communicate that knowledge in writing. By the same token, students may be able to provide the written explanation, but do not truly understand the process and are unable to represent it visually or orally. This assessment gives you a deeper understanding of students' skill and knowledge.

## 3, 2, 1

We can also use short writing assignments to check for understanding. 3, 2, 1 is a tool used to determine students' knowledge of various concepts and their interrelationships. This is a relatively simple tool. Students identify three things they know about one concept, two things about a second concept, and finally, one thing that connects the two or a question they have about the two concepts.

So, for example, the students could identify three things they know about subjects, two things they know about verbs, and one thing that connects the two or one question they have about subjects and verbs. Or they might identify three things they know about quadrilaterals, two things they know about a rhombus, and one thing that connects the two or a question related to quadrilaterals and a rhombus.

This exercise will help you know the level to which they truly understand each concept and how the concepts relate to one another, allowing you to assess their knowledge and ability to think about the interrelatedness of two different concepts.

As you review the products generated by this assessment, examine the responses for each concept and the interrelationship identified. Are the responses correct? How in-depth are they? Are the responses superficial or do they show a greater understanding? In particular, is the connection identified for the two concepts accurate, and what level of understanding does it demonstrate? If the student poses a question rather than a connection, consider what level of understanding the question demonstrates.

Group the responses by the degree of understanding they show. Use these groupings as a guide as you develop instruction. Develop more complex learning activities for those who show greater understanding, and provide greater support for those who have only a superficial understanding.

### 1-Minute Paper

In *Classroom Assessment Techniques: A Handbook for College Teachers* (1993), Thomas Angelo and Patricia Cross identify a number of techniques for quick assessments to check for understanding. Many of the assessments they identify take advantage of quick-write prompts, in which students are given three to five minutes to write anything they want about a question or topic. This can be used to gather formative assessment data. The writing can be purely free writing with no parameters, or you can use probes like these: What was the muddiest point in today's lesson? What was the clearest point today, and how could you use what you've learned?

This type of activity provides feedback that can be used to refine instruction. It is an efficient and immediate way for students to press the reset button. Review the quick writing samples generated by your students, noting misconceptions and concepts that may need to be retaught or reinforced. Rather than a detailed analysis of student performance, quick writes are designed as a quick review of student performance relative to a specific concept or lesson. You should use your findings to adjust instruction for the next lesson, addressing the issues you noted as you reviewed the students' written responses to your writing prompt.

## Weekly Summaries

For a broader perspective, have students write a weekly summary, reflecting on what they learned during the week. To prompt reflection on personal learning, ask the students to respond to the question "What did you learn personally from class discussions, activities, and readings conducted this week?" To engage the students in evaluating what they have learned and to help them transfer the knowledge they have learned to other content areas or to the "real world," ask, "How do you think what was taught this week, in class and through your readings, will work in the real world?" And finally, to support students in their development and to encourage students to use the content to transform their own perspective, ask, "How could you personally use the information?" This is an opportunity for students to engage with the material and discover what resonates with them.

Use the feedback generated by students to guide future discussion and to help students transfer what they are learning to other course work and content areas. The feedback can also help you design future instruction so that students can more easily see the relevance of the content as it relates to their personal lives.

A weekly summary can also serve as a tool for you to evaluate your instruction. The students' writing can help you see how effective the instructional strategies you have implemented during the week have been. As you review students' writing, determine if students learned the things you wanted them to learn. Determine if students understood the relevance of what you taught to other content areas and its application in the real world.

## Journaling

Journaling activities, such as double-entry journals, can be used to assess student understanding if you take the time to review the journals regularly. In a science class, you might have students journal their observations in the field or when doing lab experiments in one column, and then relate those observations to what they read in the chapter in a second column. This will not only allow you to assess where students are in their understanding, but it will also help them as they read the text.

Or in a social studies class, you might have students take notes from the textbook in the left-hand column and then record their thoughts, reactions, or connections to current events in the right-hand column. When recording their thoughts and reactions, students should make connections between the text and themselves, other books or media, or the world around them (readwritethink 2013).

Double-entry journals provide you with two sources of data from which to track student learning. In the students' notes from the text, you can examine their ability to identify key points and concepts addressed in the reading. When evaluating students' observations or reflections on the reading you can assess their ability to connect their reading to prior knowledge, other concepts, or their world.

In your review, assess students' ability to make appropriate connections or observations that clarify or explain the text. You can use the information gleaned from their journals as you work to develop students' ability to explain the content in ways that make it more understandable and relevant to them. You can also assess their ability to apply their learning to other concepts or situations.

*Timed or Free Writes*

Timed writings or free writes can be used at any point during a lesson to gain a picture of the students' current understanding of the content being taught. Students are given a prompt to respond to and a limited time frame in which to write. In an English class, students might be asked to respond to a prompt regarding a book currently being discussed in class. In a social studies or science class, students might correlate an issue being studied to current events. This provides students practice with extemporaneous writing.

Students can be given as much as thirty minutes to write, but blocks of time as short as five minutes can be used. The amount of time you provide for the activity will depend on what the writing sample will be used to evaluate and your overall learning goal for the activity. More time is not always better. Students should have sufficient time to address the question posed with appropriate detail, but not so much time that they aren't required to narrow the focus of their writing. Ideally the writing will address only one or two competencies. More time will be required if students are required to synthesize information or compare and contrast multiple issues.

Prompts should focus on specific learning outcomes. Write the prompt so that it engages students in a written dialogue about the content. Prompts should be open, with more than one possible answer. Don't write the prompt with a predefined response in mind. Make sure your question is clear, and use vocabulary with which the students should be familiar. Use content-appropriate language, as well. This will allow you to assess students' understanding of academic vocabulary related to the learning outcome to be assessed. Keep your prompts culturally relevant and appropriate; avoid insulting or stereotyping students.

In evaluating the response, look for evidence that the students understand the key concepts you are trying to teach. If the prompt is related to a reading assignment, look for evidence that supports the students' comprehension of the text. When examining literature, evaluate students' understanding of character development, setting, the relationship between the protagonist and the antagonist, and so on.

Free writes also provide an efficient tool to evaluate the student's ability to defend his or her position and provide supporting evidence. Depending on your prompt, you may be examining the student's ability to state a view and then support that opinion, the ability to implement persuasive argument, or the ability to implement metaphor to create a picture. Your learning outcome will determine the focus of your evaluation.

### Entrance and Exit Cards

Prior to beginning a new unit of instruction, a teacher may ask students to complete an "entrance card" on a question related to the unit. For example, a teacher may ask students to respond to the question "What are similes? Provide an example." The students' responses will give the teacher an idea of the students' prior knowledge and their initial questions. This can help you determine where to begin the sequence of instruction and inform your initial decisions about grouping students. Students able to provide a correct definition and example may work on a creative writing assignment, while students who lack the knowledge may receive direct instruction on similes.

Similarly, at the end of the unit you can have students complete exit cards, gathering student responses to key questions studied through the unit. For example, in a science class you might ask the students to respond to a question such as "What are the steps to the scientific method?" or "Draw a picture of a cell and label the parts."

The information from entrance cards can be used to make on-the-spot alterations to the day's lesson, and exit cards can be used to revise the next day's lesson to address those questions students still have. Additionally, the information from entrance and exit cards can be used to determine the level of student learning. Examine the type of responses students make; do these responses demonstrate a deep understanding of the content, or is it more superficial? Use these as a tool to engage the students and raise their level of comprehension.

In a biology class, you might ask the students to draw and label a cell. In assessing the exit cards you would consider the following questions: Can students draw a cell? Were they then able to label each of the parts: cell membrane, nucleus, mitochondria, vesicles, cytoplasm, golgi, ribosomes, cilium? Which ones did they miss? Were the shapes used appropriate or did they draw a circle and make a few squiggles? They can draw and label a cell, but do they know the functions of each part? Learning the connection between the function, location, and structure of each shape could be the stepping-off point for some students, taking them to another level with the content.

*Ticket Out*

Similar to an entrance or exit card, a ticket out is a short response item to which students are asked to respond in the last few minutes of a lesson. Students are given a prompt that usually requires a one- or two-word response or short statement. They hand in their response on their way out of the door. For example, in a math class you might ask the students, "What is the Pythagorean theorem?" or "Factor this quadratic: $(6x^2 + 38x + 14)$." As students leave the room, you can review their responses, evaluating their comprehension of the day's lesson or a specific concept that was taught.

A quick review of the students' responses will allow you to determine their level of comprehension as it pertains to the question posed. By selecting a question that focuses on a key concept, you will be able to utilize your analysis of their responses to expand on your instruction during the next class hour if necessary.

*ACE*

ACE is a technique used to guide how students respond to short-answer and constructed response questions. The strategy provides students with a framework to use when responding to questions designed to assess their learning. When responding to questions, students need to not only answer the question, but also back up their response with evidence. They then need to support that evidence by discussing their perspective or their personal experience, or by providing additional clarification. In reading and writing circles, ACE stands for Answer, Cite, Explain or Expand. In math settings, it stands for Answer, Compute, and Explain.

By having the students follow this step-by-step process in responding to the prompts provided, the teacher is provided with an excellent tool to help guide students' writing and to assess student knowledge of the materials that have been covered as part of the class. This technique can be utilized in coordination with free writes, journaling, and other open-ended writing assignments.

Prior to using this technique, inform the students of your expectations for their writing. Ideally, students will use key words from the posed question in their answer to the question. They should also be sure they completely answer the question. They need to support their answer with evidence from the textbook or other readings that proves or further explains their response. Finally, they need to elaborate on their response or explain the connection between their answer and the evidence, discussing their relative importance or clarifying their answer by using specific examples.

This tool will allow you to evaluate the students' level of understanding of the concept that is addressed. In evaluating student responses, attention should be paid to each part of their response. Is the answer to the question relevant and accurate? Have they cited reliable and relevant sources? Do they clearly tie their response to the sources cited as they expand on their response? Additionally, by examining the quality and depth of the students' responses, you can identify specific learning skills that students may need to further develop.

*Extended Learning Projects*

Extended learning projects are projects in which multiple points have been designated by the teacher to monitor student progress and provide substantive, constructive feedback to students about their progress. It is an activity that is designed to help students master the concepts they are demonstrating through the project. These projects are conducted over an extended period of time and typically run simultaneously with other instructional activities. The nature of these projects allows them to be an ideal formative assessment. As student progress is monitored, you are able to modify instruction to address common issues and individual learning needs one on one.

Depending on the project, checkpoints may include multiple drafts of a writing assignment, an outline, a written proposal, or a story board for a multimedia project to be developed. Formative assessment data can be gathered at each checkpoint. Information should be gathered concerning not only the students' progress but also their understanding of the concepts being addressed through the project. Develop a simple checklist to track student performance.

It is tempting with extended projects to focus on the mechanics of the project being developed. While it is important to provide students with support as they deal with the mechanics of the project, to foster student learning we need to pay attention to the students' ability to demonstrate their learning. At each checkpoint, monitor student achievement of the learning outcomes. Consider developing a simple rubric that you can use to rate student performance in relation to the outcomes. Then use these findings to support the students' mastery of the concepts through further instruction.

## IMPLEMENTATION

Student writing gives us a clear picture of their understanding of concepts and ability to communicate that understanding. Learning can be enhanced by the feedback we provide regarding their writing. The focus should be on the content being assessed, not on the writing ability of the student. Writing ability should only be assessed if it has been identified as one of the learning goals to be evaluated as part of the assessment.

It is easy to get carried away and to overrate students' content knowledge because they demonstrate strong writing skills. Likewise, it is easy to score students' content knowledge lower than it actually is when they demonstrate poor writing skills. Focus on the specific content presented. Do not make inferences about what you think the student meant just because he or she demonstrates strong writing skills.

When using writing as an assessment tool, the particular writing assignment needs to be closely aligned to specific learning objectives. In evaluating the writing sample, the focus should be on statements that clearly demonstrate the students' progress in meeting the identified objectives. In evaluating writing samples, consider underlining key statements that support your evaluation of a student's content knowledge as it relates to the objective being evaluated.

Invite students to help you develop the checklist or rubric that you will use to evaluate their writing. This will give students ownership of the assessment of the writing process, and give you insight into their understanding of the writing process as well as their content knowledge. The process of collaboratively writing assessment tools will provide you with additional information about their learning that can also be used as part of your formative assessment process. Students become motivated to meet high expectations when they have helped develop the assessment criteria (Peterson 2007).

## CONCLUSION

Writing is a life skill. In this chapter we have explored a variety of techniques that can be used to support the use of writing as an instructional tool and a formative assessment measure in multiple content areas. Writing across the curriculum has long been a practice encouraged within K–12 education because of the depth it can bring to content-specific studies. It is practiced with varying degrees of success by many educators.

The writing strategies discussed in this chapter, such as quick writes, timed writings, journals, ACE, and others can be used to integrate writing into any discipline. These tools will help students process what they have learned. As the teacher, you can then use what you learn from their writing to guide the instructional process by way of formative assessment. If writing is a consistent instructional practice in the classroom, it can be used effectively as a tool to enhance learning, as well as to assess student knowledge of the content.

# NINE
## Graphic Organizers

Graphic organizers are designed to help students and teachers organize information related to specific concepts, constructs, or processes. They are visual or graphic displays that show relationships between the elements of a concept or relationships between concepts. While graphic organizers are used primarily to teach students, they can also be used for assessment. They provide us with a tool to understand how students visualize the concepts and the relationships we are trying to teach. In this chapter we will discuss the use of graphic organizers as tools to not only support learning but to also gather data on student learning for use as formative assessments.

Graphic organizers and advance organizers can help students better understand the relationship between concepts and the flow of information. By having students fill in missing information as we lecture, we can quickly tell if they are following the flow of the presentation and understanding the concepts.

We can also build these advance organizers with varying levels of complexity, allowing us to modify instruction to better provide instruction based on students' individual performance level. We can design highly detailed advance organizers that are missing limited amounts of information, for students of lower ability to complete. Less detailed advance organizers, requiring more information to be filled in, can be created for students of higher ability.

### STRUCTURE TO SUPPORT USE AS A FORMATIVE ASSESSMENT

To serve effectively as a formative assessment tool, the graphic organizer should be tied closely to a specific objective or learning goal. The use of the graphic organizer needs to be focused, and clear directions also need to be provided. The knowledge of the students as it relates to the objective or learning goal should be assessed, rather than their ability to follow directions.

## GRAPHIC ORGANIZERS

Graphic organizers come in a variety of formats, each with a different instructional purpose. In this section we look specifically at graphic organizers that can help students organize vocabulary, examine relationships between two or more concepts, look at hierarchical relationships, or map characteristics. We will look at the use of graphic organizers to support not only instruction but also assessment. By understanding how our students see the concepts we are teaching and the relationships that are present, we will be able to address misconceptions and identify underlying issues that are keeping students from progressing in the domain.

### Cloze

The cloze procedure is similar to a technique used by *MAD* magazine and others to engage readers in creating a funny story. *MAD* magazine produced stories that were missing key words throughout the story—blanks were inserted instead. These are commonly known as Mad Libs. Each blank was identified by part of speech: noun, verb, adjective, adverb, and so on. For example:

I went to the _____(place) with _____(name), _____(name), and _____(name). It was a _____(adjective) time. While we were there we _____(verb) from _____(noun) and _____(verb) with a(n) _____(noun). When we got home _____(pronoun) were _____ (adjective).

The technique used for educational purposes focuses on the student's ability to complete a written passage using correct terminology. You can also use the cloze technique to assess the student's ability to comprehend specific concepts or recall relevant information related to a piece of writing or construct. The cloze technique is a common reading assessment, but it also can be used to assess student comprehension and understanding of a given text. It can also be used to assess the student's vocabulary and knowledge of a given subject and his or her ability to think critically and analytically about a subject.

To develop a cloze document, words are deleted from a selected passage and replaced with blanks. Ideally, the deleted words are key to understanding the concept or the meaning of a selected text. A word-count formula may also be used to simply remove words from the text, requiring students to recall the text and replace the missing words. After selecting a grade-appropriate text, leave the first and last sentence intact and remove selected text. To assess knowledge of the topic or the students' ability to use semantic cues, delete content words that carry meaning specific to the concept being evaluated.

In the final draft of the document, make all of the blanks equal in length to avoid including visual clues about the length of the word omitted. Have students read the entire passage before beginning to fill in the blanks. When creating a cloze document, you can modify the technique by including a list of suggested words to put in each blank or by including the first letter of each missing word but providing no word suggestions.

Students should be sure to read the completed passage, using this as a tool to self-assess their own understanding by making sure the completed passage is correct and understandable. When you assess the completed passage, accept any reasonable word response. Make sure that the completed assessment demonstrates a clear understanding of the text or concept being evaluated. Identify misunderstandings when words are utilized that create a logical sentence but do not demonstrate a clear understanding of the concept being assessed.

*Advance Organizers*

Advance organizers are used to demonstrate the relationship of two or more concepts or the interrelationships between elements that define a specific concept. These are typically used to help students gain an understanding of how various things are related. When used after teaching a concept, an advance organizer can be used to assess student understanding of the relationships. There are a number of formats used to develop graphic organizers, including herringbone, cycle charts, hierarchical charts, or organizational tables.

*Affinity Diagram*

Affinity diagrams can be used to expose misunderstandings and to strengthen understanding of key concepts. Developing an affinity diagram involves engaging students, first in a brainstorming session to create a list of information and ideas related to a specific topic. Second, students sort the list into holistic groups. Finally, each of these groups is titled and organized into a diagram that demonstrates hierarchy or relationship.

This activity could be utilized in a history class to examine students' understanding of economics. For example, students may be asked, "Given what we know of economics, what are the factors that are influencing the current economy?" As a class, the students brainstorm a list of historic factors. They may do this with a computer program, on a whiteboard or flip chart, or with sticky notes that are easy to rearrange and organize.

Once the list is created and is fairly exhaustive, the items are grouped into clusters of related information. Title each cluster with a common name that describes the grouping and then draw connecting lines using directional arrows indicating relationships. Line the clusters up if you need to show a hierarchical relationship.

In assessing an affinity diagram, observe individual and group performance. Consider the individual's ability to contribute to the discussion, from brainstorming to organization. Is the student able to identify appropriate factors related to the economy? Are contributions limited to those discussed in class, or are other factors identified? Are the factors identified complex or more simple and easily identified? Are the factors organized and related to one another logically and appropriately?

This can be completed as a whole class discussion, in small groups, or individually. How it is completed depends on your intent. If you want a clear understanding of individual performance, the students could complete this activity as individuals. Attention to and monitoring of student performance during group discussion is needed to gather more than a holistic perspective when assessing individual performance in a group setting. It is a valid desire, however, to gain an overview of the understanding of a group of students. When using an affinity diagram created by the group, be sure to take notice of students who do not understand the concepts or are unable to participate in the discussion.

## Memory Matrix

Another graphic organizer that is useful as a formative assessment tool is a memory matrix. It can be used to assess students' understanding of related concepts. A memory matrix is simply a table that indicates specific concepts across the top, divided into columns. Within each column, characteristics of each concept are identified. The matrix consists of specific concepts (for example, types of plants) listed in the row across the top, with characteristics of the concepts listed down the columns on the side. Students then match the plant with the appropriate characteristics. Matrices can be developed in which students compare different mathematical formulas and their purposes, types of writing, works by various authors and theorists, and so on. A Spanish language teacher may use a memory matrix to assess the students' ability to conjugate -*ir* and -*ar* verbs. Each row would identify the forms for *yo, tu, usted, nosotros,* and *ustedes.* To develop a memory matrix, create a table inserting appropriate row and column headings, leaving the cells blank. Set a time limit based on the complexity of the matrix, instructing students to fill in the blank cells.

When assessing the matrices, look for patterns. Consider the students' level of understanding. Are there certain characteristics in which they demonstrate limited understanding? Where did they do particularly

| conj \ verb | hablar | comer | vivir |
|---|---|---|---|
| yo | | | |
| tu | | | |
| usted | habla | | |
| nosotros | | comemos | |
| ustedes | | | viven |

**Figure 9.1.  Spanish Verbs**

well? You may include as many rows and columns as you like. The purpose is to assess the students' recall of information and their ability to categorize it.

*Character Mapping*

A character map is a diagram that is used to compare the traits of characters within a story or an event. Character maps are typically used in language arts classes, but they can also be employed in other content classes such as history, science, art, music, or even math, as we look at characters who participated in various events related to the content area.

Character mapping, in which a character from a novel or nonfiction work is placed in a middle circle with his or her characteristics placed around the circle like spokes of a wheel, can also be used to assess understanding. Each character is identified in a separate diagram in the center. The spokes are labeled with characteristics that describe the character.

This technique can be used to have students simply identify the characteristics of each character in a story. Or it can be used to separate characteristics that are directly identified within the story and those inferred by the reader. When considering real-life characters, the characteristics can be identified as those that are fact and those that are opinion. A character map is used to assess students' understanding of character development within a given text.

*Concept Mapping*

A concept map is very similar to a character map, but rather than looking at character traits, the diagram shows the relationship between concepts. Concept maps give you a tool to assess how well students see the bigger picture and the connections between concepts. A concept map is a visual representation to help identify relationships between concepts within a specific body of knowledge. Their value is in the fact that they are not linear and can help students better visualize the interrelationships that exist between concepts that are not linear or hierarchical. A concept map is a simple diagram of interconnected constructs that are linked with directional lines.

A topic is placed in the middle of the diagram, and students brainstorm information related to the concept to create a wheel of information. The relationship between concepts can be clarified by using linking phrases such as "gives rise to," "results in," "is required by," or "contributes to." The process of concept mapping can reveal "unanticipated structure," providing us with an understanding of how our students perceive the content being taught and how the concepts are related.

Additionally, there is the occasional "aha" moment, when your students and you yourself might see the concepts differently than you ever have before, providing new understandings to you and your students—as in the example in figure 9.2, where students made connections between rocks that were originally formed as sedimentary or igneous rocks and were transformed through heat and pressure into metamorphic rocks.

Originally developed to enhance learning in the sciences, a concept map originates with an explicit key idea or focused question. Concept maps reflect recall of information related to the specific concept or question and facilitate making sense of the intra- and interrelationships within

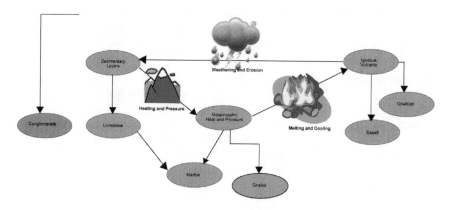

**Figure 9.2.   Concept Map of the Rock Cycle**

the subject. Interrelationships within concept-rich subjects frequently do not become evident until all of the concepts have been introduced. Developing an understanding of how concepts interrelate will help your students in their understanding of higher-order concepts and the interrelationship of those concepts.

Concept maps also help in the transfer of their knowledge to subsequent units of instruction. They encourage students to adopt a deep/holistic approach, allowing them to better understand the concepts being taught.

We can also teach students to develop concept maps to monitor their own metacognition. According to Ausubel (1970), meaningful learning takes place when it is related to a learner's own prior knowledge. This can be facilitated by linking these concepts into the existing cognitive knowledge structure of the students. New ideas can be categorized under the broader overall concept and links identified to other concepts, making structural relations clearer, as in the relationships between rock structure and deposits of natural gas. Assimilation of concepts into existing frameworks helps students visualize relationships and build mental models, presenting a two-dimensional view of a content area or unit of instruction.

Not only does a concept map allow students to identify the major concepts, but it also allows them to demonstrate the interrelationships between those ideas. When new concepts are introduced, students frequently revert to rote memorization and make no attempt to relate the concepts to one another. The new information remains surface learning and is not integrated with their existing understanding of the content and made relevant for them to retain. For example, a colleague's eighth-grade math students learned about metrics in math class. Yet, two weeks later when the science teacher started a unit using metrics, the students did not recall that they were even familiar with the metric system. They were unable to apply even the simplest measures that they had just mastered in math class.

When using concept maps as a formative assessment measure, we should consider the depth, breadth, and accuracy of the students' understanding. We need to pay specific attention to the interrelationships they identify between constructs, and their ability to accurately portray those connections. Do they understand the basic framework of geology? Do they know how sedimentary, metamorphic, and igneous rocks are related to one another?

A student may have a firm knowledge of the key ideas that make up an event, issue, or concept, but they may not understand the finer connections between the constructs that make up that event, issue, or concept. Do they understand how the geologic makeup of the land contributes to the availability of groundwater?

Use concept maps to delve more deeply into the learners' understanding. Use this information to design activities that will stretch the understanding of those students who have a clear knowledge of the interconnections within a field, as well as activities that will help other students develop the depth and breadth of their understanding—in this case, exploring the impact of geology on the local economy and the availability of water.

*Describing Wheel*

A describing wheel is similar to a concept map. With a describing wheel, the concept is placed in the middle of the wheel. A larger circle outside of the wheel is divided into sections. A statement describing a concept is placed in each section of the wheel. Younger students could draw pictures describing the concept.

In evaluating a describing wheel, the focus again is on the ability of the learner to describe the characteristics of the concept. The level of the responses should be taken into consideration. Consider the depth of understanding the descriptions represent; do they demonstrate a superficial understanding of the concept or a more in-depth knowledge? Are the responses accurate? Do the students demonstrate a narrow understanding or do the descriptions indicate a breadth of knowledge?

*Fact and Opinion*

A fact and opinion graphic organizer is a two-column chart. The topic being reviewed is at the top of the two columns. In the first column, students list facts about the topic. In the second column, they write opinions. The purpose of this tool is to help the students understand the difference between fact and opinion.

In a health science class, the topic "Marijuana is a safe drug" could be placed at the top of chart. The left-hand column would be labeled "Fact" and the right-hand column would be labeled "Opinion." Students would list in the first column facts about marijuana, such as it is made from the *Cannabis sativa* plant; it contains THC (delta-9-tetrahydrocannabinol); THC is a "mind-altering" chemical; according to a 2012 NIDA study, 6.5 percent of eighth graders had used marijuana in the previous month; and so on. In the second column, students would list opinions they had researched on marijuana, such as marijuana is a safe drug; everyone uses marijuana; legalizing marijuana ignores health dangers; and so on.

In analyzing this assessment, attention should be paid to the accuracy of the items listed in each column. Consider the following questions: Are the items listed assigned to the appropriate column? Are they accurate? What level of critical thinking do the facts and opinions that are listed demonstrate? Do the listed items demonstrate an in-depth understanding of the research, or are they superficial—gleaned from unreliable resources?

## Who, What, When, Where, and Why

Who, what, when, where, and why have long been the standard of journalistic writing. They also provide a foundation for reviewing issues related to a specific content area. As students learn to evaluate and discuss issues in science, history, English, foreign language study, and other courses of study, it is important that they look at the whole issue—understanding the who, what, when, where, and why of the issue and not just their sole perception.

In having the students complete an analysis of an issue using who, what, when, where, and why, the teacher can analyze the depth of the students' understanding of the issue. In this simple activity, a table is made with rows labeled Who, What, When, Where, and Why. The issue is written at the top of the table. In the space provided the student responds to each probe describing in a succinct manner the specific details that describe the issue and address the question.

In reviewing the completed product, the teacher should pay attention to the accuracy of information provided and the level of detail. Consider the following questions: Is the student able to respond with succinct, clear responses? Or are the responses wordy, talking around the issue rather than clearly addressing the point? Do the responses indicate a high level of understanding or only a superficial understanding? Correlate the responses to the learning outcomes to be evaluated and determine if they demonstrate the degree of understanding and knowledge that the student needs to achieve.

## Persuasion Map

A persuasion map provides a good outline for writing a persuasive paper or developing the initial arguments for a debate. It provides a tool from which the teacher can observe the students' ability to develop an argument. A persuasion map is developed horizontally. On the left side of the page the hypothesis is stated. To the right of the hypothesis, three reasons that support the hypothesis are listed. To the right of each reason, three facts or examples are listed that support each reason.

For example, in a science class the following diagram might be developed (see figure 9.3).

In evaluating each map, consider the accuracy and level of each argument. Do the reasons that are identified actually support the hypothesis? Do the facts and examples support the reason presented? What level of critical thinking do the reasons and examples demonstrate? Do they demonstrate depth and/or breadth, as they look at the concept being studied?

| Hypothesis: | Reasons which support hypothesis | Facts/examples which support each reason. |
|---|---|---|
| | 1. | a. |
| | | b. |
| | | c. |
| | 2. | a. |
| | | b. |
| | | c. |
| | 3. | a. |
| | | b. |
| | | c. |

**Figure 9.3.   Science Persuasion Map**

Is a superficial argument presented or does the presented information demonstrate a strong understanding of the issue being argued?

*Venn Diagram*

A Venn diagram consists of two or more interlocking circles, representing two or more concepts. It is used to demonstrate the student's understanding regarding the similarities and differences between the concepts. To develop a Venn diagram, the characteristics of each concept are identified. The characteristics that the concepts share are placed in the space where the circles overlap. The characteristics that apply to only the individual concept is placed out in the circle, separate from the other concept circle.

When evaluating Venn diagrams, it is important to pay attention to the accuracy of the characteristics that the student identified for each concept. Do the characteristics accurately portray each concept? Once the veracity of the characteristics is assessed, evaluate the student's ability to identify similarities and differences between the two concepts. Again, attention should be paid to the depth of understanding and the knowledge that is demonstrated. Determine the degree to which the provided characteristics demonstrate an in-depth understanding of the concept.

*KWL*

KWL assessments have been around for a number of years and are frequently used by teachers. KWL is traditionally a three-step process, although there are some variations that will increase the length of the process. KWL stands for "Know," "Want to know," and "Learned." At its very basic level, at the beginning of a unit or extended learning activity, you work through an individual or group process in which students identify what they already know about the content and what else they want to know about the content. To bring it full circle, you complete this activity by having the students identify what they have learned.

When having individual students complete the task, have the students fold a sheet of paper into three columns, lengthwise, labeling the first column "Know," the middle column "Want to know," and the final column "Learned." This can also be completed as a whole group with either the teacher or a student serving as scribe for the entire class, writing responses on the whiteboard in the appropriate column. Or for individual accountability, students can write their ideas on sticky notes, and post those on the whiteboard in the appropriate column.

The teacher and students work to identify what they already know and what they want to know. As an introductory activity, the students complete the first two columns and use this information to help complete the design of the unit of instruction. This will allow you to make the unit more personally relevant to the students and develop more engaging activities. You will find that you will be able to quickly see what the students already know and also their areas of interest. You will also be able to find the holes in their knowledge bank by seeing what areas of the content they did not identify.

This can be used to introduce a unit as a preassessment and then follow up at the end of the unit reflecting with students on what they have learned. For example, you might have students complete a KWL chart for the U.S. legislative system.

This assessment allows you to not only identify what students already know about the content to be taught, but also to learn about what they want to know. KWL charts provide a wonderful tool for engaging your students in the content to be taught because of this "buy-in" aspect. By giving you an understanding of what the students already know and want to learn, this data can be used to design instruction to build on that knowledge and address the students' interests. Use this information to take your students beyond even their own expectations.

There are a number of variations. KNL stands for "What Do I Know," "What Do I Need to Learn," and "What Have I Learned." There's also KWL + Reflection, in which at the end of a unit or learning activity students are asked to reflect on what they have learned during the entire KWL process. There is also KWL + "How Will I Use This Information," in which students focus on how what they have learned transfers to the real world, other content areas, or the next unit of instruction.

As you analyze student responses to this activity, consider not only the accuracy but also the breadth and depth of their responses. Do they have a broad understanding of the U.S. legislative system or is it narrow,

| UNITED STATED LEGISLATIVE SYSTEM | | |
| --- | --- | --- |
| **KNOW** | **WANT TO KNOW** | **LEARNED** |
| House | How do the legislators decide how to vote? | |
| Senate | | |
| Members of the house and senate make up laws | Can individual citizens suggest laws? How? | |
| Lobbyists impact the vote | How come some legislators stay in office forever? | |
| President can veto | What is my role in the legislative system? | |
| | Can the president veto parts of a bill? | |
| | How does the Executive Branch interface with the Legislative branch? | |

**Figure 9.4.  KWL: United States Legislative System**

within confined areas? Consider how much students really know. Not only is this information apparent in their responses to "What Do I Know," it also is evident in their ability to identify what they want to know. Do they know enough about the legislative system to be able to name things they would like to know more about? Or is their knowledge level so shallow they cannot even identify additional things about which they would like to know more? By knowing what information students bring to the learning experience, you will be able to address the subject matter to the breadth or depth needed to increase their understanding of the content.

Be aware that students' responses could also be an indicator of motivation. Consider whether your students' responses are governed by their lack of motivation rather than their actual knowledge. Perhaps you will need to include activities designed to gain your students' attention and raise their awareness of the importance of the content to be addressed.

The final phase of the KWL chart requires that we address the question, what did they learn? When students participate in this assessment of their own learning, retention is enhanced. Too frequently, teachers stop short, completing only the beginning of this activity, having students identify what they know and what they want to know, but leaving off the final summation "What I Have Learned."

Reflection is an effective tool to ensure learning. When students reflect on what they have learned, they will be able to recall it and apply it at a future time much more easily. This opportunity to reflect on their learning will not only help students retain the information taught, it will also help them process what they learned and make connections to other things that they know. By using the entire KWL process, you will be able to assess where students are in their learning, correct misconceptions, close holes in their understanding, and facilitate the retention of the new information they have learned in your class.

## IMPLEMENTATION

Selectively review the graphic organizers you use to support instruction. Remember that you do not need to track every piece of data available to you. Select the information you wish to log. Make the selection based upon its relationship to the learning outcome. In evaluating graphic organizers, pay attention to three key factors: (1) Is the information presented by the student accurate? (2) At what level does the student respond to the probes presented? Does the presented information demonstrate an in-depth understanding or a superficial understanding of the concepts presented? (3) Are the relationships that are suggested by the graphic organizer accurate? Again, do the presented relationships demonstrate an in-depth understanding or a superficial understanding?

Use the information gleaned from reviewing the advance organizers that are completed by the students to revise your instruction. Consider providing additional support for students who do not demonstrate a clear understanding of the concepts being taught. If students are advanced, provide opportunities for them to gain further knowledge and move ahead with course material or learn more about the concepts being revisited by other students.

## CONCLUSION

Graphic organizers are tools that work well to help students learn to organize content and show relationships between concepts. Select the advance organizer you use based upon your instructional or assessment purpose; determine whether you want to understand how students view the relationship between constructs or if they understand the hierarchical relationship. Each will require a different type of advance organizer.

Rather than relying on narrative, advance organizers allow students to demonstrate their understanding of the content visually. They allow students who may not be able to describe their thinking to actually show their thinking. Graphic organizers bring a level of clarity that can easily be missed in a narrative presentation. Since they work well as a tool to support instruction, it becomes just a matter of taking the time to examine the result of the learning activity to gather formative assessment data.

# TEN

## Games

Formative assessment involves careful planning and the selection of learning activities and opportunities to be used during instruction that can be utilized to support the formative assessment process. Games that are designed to foster student interaction with the content and the explanation of constructs by the students can be used as measures to support formative assessment. Games provide a low-stress option that supports risk taking.

Games can also support the learner as they step out on the educational ledge and demonstrate their knowledge and skills in ways that we may not see in more traditional assessment settings. Traditional assessments may possibly be outside of the students' comfort zone. In this chapter we will discuss the use of "game show" games as a formative assessment tool. Specific games will be described, with detailed information for implementing each in the learning environment.

### STRUCTURE TO SUPPORT USE AS A FORMATIVE ASSESSMENT

To be used effectively as a tool to support formative assessment, the game needs to be closely tied to the learning objectives. The questions used in the game need to be focused and have a clear tie to those objectives. To track individual performance you will need to monitor individual as well as group performance during the game. Create a log sheet similar to the one described earlier in the text to track individual performance. Students also need to be comfortable in a fun, competitive learning environment that supports risk taking and does not judge students for incorrect responses.

## GAMES

There is no reason that formative assessment should not be fun; games provide a wonderful tool to engage the students with the content in a low-threat environment. This mirrors the video game environment, in which students are able to press the reset button and take the opportunity to go back and learn.

We can use games to assess student progress, and then use our findings to help students address the learning gaps that are present. The most important tool that games will provide in the formative assessment process is the ability to give students immediate feedback regarding their progress. With games, the weak areas in a student's preparation will be immediately evident.

### *Jeopardy*

An old favorite, Jeopardy provides a fun way to engage students. Jeopardy is a reverse trivia game, with questions phrased as answers and answers as questions (Hitton 2013). Templates are available online using PowerPoint or Flash to create your own Jeopardy game. Given a good template, you will need to identify appropriate categories and develop questions that align with the content being assessed through the game. Questions to be included in each category need to be of progressive difficulty, each question being somewhat more difficult than the previous.

When designing a Jeopardy game, first identify the learning outcomes to be assessed through the game. Each learning outcome can be used as the basis for one or more of the six categories used in the standard format for Jeopardy. Using a different outcome to define each category will give you an overview of student learning. For a more in-depth evaluation of student knowledge, each learning outcome can be broken down into its elements, and each indicator can be used as the theme for a category, defining two, three, or even all six categories.

To write questions for your Jeopardy game, begin with the easiest level (Hitton 2013). Write a simple question that aligns with your first category. Then write a statement that describes the answer to the question. This statement will become the question in Jeopardy, and your original question will be the answer.

Keep your initial questions concrete, with a clear alignment between the description and the question it describes. Often, to make a question more difficult you only need to select a more obscure fact or abstract characteristic to describe the question you are using. Verify your questions and answers, making sure that in developing an engaging game you are not teaching your students incorrect information through the game. Jeopardy requires at least two sources for a question before it can be used on the show (Hitton 2013).

To play the game, divide the class into teams. If your class is large, run more than one Jeopardy game at the same time. The larger the teams, the more likely students are going to be able to fade into the background and become a classroom management issue rather than an active participant. In Jeopardy, there are typically three players. If you have enough computers, you can have teams of three play the game against each other. If not, divide the class into teams with three or four players on each team.

You can create teams comprising as many as five players. Beyond five players, it is too easy for students not to participate. You can also increase the number of "players" by having five or six teams playing against one another. Rather than trying to formatively assess student learning during the game, have students record their response to each question, and use these recording sheets to assess student learning. Since these recording sheets will not be used to assign a grade, other than participation, students should not feel the need to cheat and record their response after the question has been answered correctly.

## Password

Password is a game that works well for reviewing vocabulary (Szeto 2010). The game is designed to be played by teams of two, one team pitted against another. One member of the team gives clues to the other team member so that they can guess the correct word. Typically a team has a limited time frame, usually one minute, to correctly name as many words as possible. The team that correctly names the most words wins.

The game can be modified for classroom use to reinforce new vocabulary words and assess the students' ability to use the terminology accurately in a sentence. The play rotates between teams after each word. To use Password as a formative assessment, you will need to implement a scoring scheme that can be used to track performance.

To utilize Password as an assessment tool, first create a list of vocabulary words associated with the objectives you have identified. Write each word on a separate 3x5 card. Create enough sets of cards so that all students can play the game at the same time. Identify groups of three or four students. If there are four students in a group, pair students in each group into separate teams. Each round, one student in the team will provide clues to the vocabulary word and the other will guess. If there are only three students in each group, students will take turns providing clues to one another.

Use timers, making sure that the students don't get bogged down on one vocabulary word and lose interest. Give students no more than thirty seconds to name each vocabulary word. If the partner names the word correctly, the team gets one point. If the student can also use the word in a sentence, the team earns an additional two points. As students play, the teacher should walk around and track each team's progress, making sure that the students are accurately recording their scores. Those scores will give you an understanding of the students' ability to use the terminology correctly and their understanding of the meaning of each vocabulary word.

## Who Wants to Be a Millionaire

Who Wants to Be a Millionaire is a quiz game that uses multiple choice questions to challenge students. To develop the game, you will write a series of multiple choice questions. These questions need to align with the learning outcomes to be assessed. Each question should have four possible answers. Questions should also be of varying levels of difficulty.

Each round begins with easier questions, with questions getting progressively more difficult the longer a student remains in the "hot seat." To help the game move quickly, create a PowerPoint presentation with each question on a separate screen. Also, remember that you need to write questions for multiple tracks. Every time a new student takes the "hot seat," you need to begin at level 1 and work up to the more difficult questions.

When using Who Wants to Be a Millionaire as a learning activity, a student earns the right to take the "hot seat" by answering the first question correctly. The winning student takes the "hot seat." Once play begins, the student remains in the "hot seat" until he or she misses a question. There are three lifelines available to students to help them identify the correct answer. They may ask a friend in the group, ask the audience or whole group, or eliminate two incorrect answers, giving them a 50/50 chance to select the correct answer. Once a lifeline has been used by a player, it is no longer available to that player. As the difficulty of the questions increases, the number of points that the question is worth increases. The final question, number 15, is worth a figurative million dollars.

During the play, all students need to record their responses to each question. At the conclusion of the game, collect the student responses, paying attention to the accuracy of the responses recorded by each student. Identify areas of weakness and provide students with specific feedback regarding their performance. This game can be fast paced, and it is a fun way to engage the students in a quick review of the content being studied. Involving the entire class in the game would be made easier if students used clickers (personal response systems) to select their choice for the correct answer to each question. The system automatically records and scores the response for each student.

## What's My Line?

The original game show *What's My Line?* ran from 1950 to 1967 in the United States (Wikipedia 2013). Three individuals, two pretenders and one person who had an interesting occupation or background, came before a panel. The panel asked the players yes/no questions, gathering information collectively, trying to figure out who was the "real" person and who were the pretenders. As long as a panelist received "yes" responses to their question they could continue asking questions. When they received a "no" response, the play passed to the next panelist.

To play the game, assign students specific historical characters or concepts they will role-play as they each have the opportunity to take on that persona for their classmates to identify. In a science class, students could become an element on the periodic table. In a language arts class, they could be a character from a book or a part of speech. In a math class, they could be a famous mathematician, a formula, or a type of equation. Evaluate student learning based on their ability to role-play their persona and on the student panelist's ability to correctly identify another student's persona.

The game can be played as a whole group activity or in teams. As a whole class activity, class members would take turns asking players questions about the persona one of them has prepared to role-play. The job of the players is to confuse the class, keeping them from identifying which student is really the identified persona. Students earn points by correctly identifying the persona being role-played by a fellow student.

Student learning can be assessed by observing the types of questions they ask to identify the persona. As you score the student panelist, evaluate his or her ability to ask logical questions that align with the persona being role-played. Also, evaluate the player's ability to accurately answer questions.

## Dictionary Deception

Dictionary Deception is a word game in which words are selected from the vocabulary covered in a particular unit to assess student knowledge. Ideally, select words that you are fairly sure the students don't know the definition of. In science, English, and language courses, students learn how to figure out the meaning of terms using suffixes, prefixes, and cognates.

Dictionary Deception is a great game to use to assess the student's ability to figure out the meaning of unfamiliar terms using the cognitive techniques that have been taught in class. Dictionary Deception is based on the board game Balderdash. This game works well as a whole class activity or in small groups. The group is presented with a list of terms for which they do not know the definition.

First, have the students review the list of words and make up definitions for each word. Second, collect the definitions and compile the definitions for each word, making sure the correct definition is on the list and that there are no duplications. Then read them, one by one, to the students. Finally, reread the list of definitions to the students. As the definitions are reread, students vote individually for the definition they believe is the correct one.

The game is scored individually, with students earning a point for each correct definition they identify. Students also earn a point when someone selects their fake definition as the true meaning of the word. The student with the most points wins. The quality of fake definitions created by the student, as well as his or her ability to identify the true definition, can both serve as indicators of the student's ability to utilize linguistic clues to determine the meaning of a word.

This is a fairly simple game, but in reviewing the definitions created by the students you will be able to determine their prior knowledge for the content to be taught, their understanding of prefixes and suffixes common to the content area you are teaching, and their ability to extrapolate from root words with which they are already familiar.

Games are great to engage students, but it can be difficult to track performance. Develop an easy checklist or log that you can use during the game to track student performance, such as the one shown in figure 10.1. Use this information to identify students who already have skill with the content, or who can use their skills with other content to develop logical and reasonable definitions for the vocabulary used in the game. Do they have a clear understanding of the terminology used? Were the definitions they wrote correct? Or were they able to identify the correct definition when they heard it?

*Pictionary*

Pictionary is similar to Password in many respects, but it takes advantage of the participant's creative skills while reviewing vocabulary. This game works well with teams of three to five individuals or as a whole class activity. It is, however, easier to maintain the attention of all students if smaller teams are formed. Each team will need a whiteboard or easel. Each team is given a vocabulary word.

One individual draws a picture representing the term, while the rest of the team guesses the word. Teams have one minute to guess the correct word. The game is designed for teams to take turns playing. With a large class, this may make the play too slow. If the class is too large, divide the class into smaller teams and set up separate games to be played simultaneously, with two teams pitted against one another. You could also design the games to be played in a tournament format. The winning teams play against each other until a winner is declared. The

| Student Name: | Vocabulary Words | | | | | |
|---|---|---|---|---|---|---|
| | Genomic | DNA | RNA | Amino Acids | Oncogenes | Mutation |
| **Peter** | I R C ☐☐☐ | I R C ☐☐☐ | I R C ☐☐☐ | I R C ☐☐☐ | I R C ☐☐☐ | I R C ☐☐☐ |
| **Susan** | I R C ☐☐☐ | I R C ☐☐☐ | I R C ☐☐☐ | I R C ☐☐☐ | I R C ☐☐☐ | I R C ☐☐☐ |
| **Larry** | I R C ☐☐☐ | I R C ☐☐☐ | I R C ☐☐☐ | I R C ☐☐☐ | I R C ☐☐☐ | I R C ☐☐☐ |
| **Maria** | I R C ☐☐☐ | I R C ☐☐☐ | I R C ☐☐☐ | I R C ☐☐☐ | I R C ☐☐☐ | I R C ☐☐☐ |
| **Patricia** | I R C ☐☐☐ | I R C ☐☐☐ | I R C ☐☐☐ | I R C ☐☐☐ | I R C ☐☐☐ | I R C ☐☐☐ |
| **Jorge** | I R C ☐☐☐ | I R C ☐☐☐ | I R C ☐☐☐ | I R C ☐☐☐ | I R C ☐☐☐ | I R C ☐☐☐ |

I = Incorrect, R = Reasonable Definition but Incorrect, C = Correct

**Figure 10.1.  Checklist for Dictionary Deception**

losing teams continue to play against each other, making sure everyone is involved.

Evaluate student learning using two factors: the accuracy of the images used to guide teammates to the correct response and the team's ability to identify the correct vocabulary word or concept. This game gives you a basic overview of students' knowledge of the vocabulary and concepts as well as their creativity. As you supervise play, monitor each student's performance, tracking student progress on a simple class score sheet. Or you can have students keep score for their team. Give students two points for being able to draw images that appropriately represent the concept and one point for correctly identifying the term.

*PowerPoint Games*

A number of games have been developed using PowerPoint. Simply search "PowerPoint game templates" in your favorite search engine. Downloading a number of these games will provide you with a quick resource for developing a review/formative assessment opportunity to do with your students. Games such as the ones discussed above, as well as Trivial Pursuit, Survivor, Concentration, and Wheel of Fortune, are all wonderful formats that can be used to develop an in-class game. If implemented appropriately, just about any game can be used to engage students with the content and monitor the progress of student learning while they play.

## IMPLEMENTATION

Often teachers try to use games as an easy review activity. They are usually designed so that the whole class plays the same game at the same time. Problems occur when students get bored. It's hard to pay attention until it's your team's turn. This can easily become a classroom management issue rather than an opportunity to have some fun while learning. The other problem is individual accountability. The larger the team, the more difficult it is to monitor individual participation. With larger teams, it becomes easier for a student to hide and let the other team members respond to the questions.

Games can be valuable tools to support student learning while assessing their learning at the same time. In implementing games in the classroom, it is important that steps be taken to make sure that all students are comfortable with the game and that the competitive nature of the game does not hinder learning (Hudson and Bristow 2006). You can build on students' inherent competitive nature, but make sure that all participants are willing participants. Do not push students to take on roles within the game that make them uncomfortable. Let students "want" to play; do not push them beyond their own willingness to participate.

When you discuss questions, focus on why an answer is correct rather than on who got a question right or wrong. Keep the competitive nature of the activity in a positive light. At the beginning of the game, review the rules of the game with the students, even though the game may be familiar to them. This will reduce arguments over the rules and how the game should be played. Use games as an opportunity to encourage student-to-student interaction and to support the development of a learning environment that supports team learning.

After the game, engage the students in a group discussion about the correct and incorrect answers. This provides you the opportunity to engage students in reflection on the content and on what they learned during the game. It is also a chance to extend learning, providing additional information about the concepts and learning outcomes that are addressed. Keep the focus on the content, rather than on individual student performance.

Games make for a relaxed environment in which to assess student learning, while maintaining that environment through the discussion. Work to build a classroom environment in which students are not judged but are allowed to participate, have fun, and learn. It is possible to have fun while learning is occurring and performance data are being gathered, so that learning can be enhanced.

## CONCLUSION

Games provide an ideal tool for assessment because students do not see the game as being a test. They can relax and enjoy the game without worrying about their individual performance. Games can serve three roles in the classroom, all at the same time. For some students, the game will serve as a review of the content, and for other students it will serve as a learning tool. They will learn content they may not have already learned. For all students, the game can serve as a tool to formatively assess their learning.

This chapter focused on the implementation of "game show" games, not educational software designed to be completed independently. Game shows such as Jeopardy, Password, Who Wants to Be a Millionaire, What's My Line?, and Pictionary and board games like Balderdash can be used to engage students while assessing their content knowledge.

When using games designed to play in small groups as a whole class, it is important to develop log sheets that can be used to track student performance. You should be able to record scores quickly, recording observations regarding student performance by using a rubric. Code scores so that you can reflect on student strengths and weaknesses at a later time. Or have students record their responses so that you can evaluate their individual performance after the game. Use the data to inform the instructional decisions you will make as you provide further instruction based on the assessed outcomes.

Video games can also be used for formative assessment purposes. Educational games that involve students in problem solving, role-play, or action can be used to support instruction and assessment. Computer-based games that automatically track student performance, adjust game play based upon student performance, and provide real-time feedback can be a great addition to the classroom, supporting teaching, learning, and assessment. Whatever the format, games provide an ideal tool to engage students and to assess their learning in a safe environment.

# ELEVEN

## Discussions

Lecture is one of the most popular instructional tools used in the secondary setting. If lecture is made interactive, incorporating discussion questions, students can be engaged and learning can be enhanced. The resulting classroom discussion can also be used to support formative assessment. Key to using discussion as a formative assessment tool is monitoring student understanding and the level of their responses. In this chapter we will discuss a number of methods that can be utilized to support the use of interactive lecture and discussion to gather formative assessment data.

### STRUCTURE TO SUPPORT USE AS A FORMATIVE ASSESSMENT

In organizing a discussion to be used as a formative assessment tool, it is important to preselect questions to guide the discussion. When outlining questions to be used for formative assessment purposes, focus on one learning objective at a time. Develop questions that get to the heart of the issue and that require students to step outside of their comfort zone. Avoid questions that require little more than short-term memory. Go beyond simple recall, and work to deepen their understanding of the content and reveal the depth of their understanding.

Develop questions that engage students and require them to apply what they've learned. For example, you might ask a question like "What if the atomic bomb had never been invented and Hiroshima and Nagasaki, Japan, had not been bombed at the end of World War II? How would the United States and the world be different now?"

Then follow up with questions designed to assess students' understanding of related concepts, thereby assessing the students' ability to research and apply critical thinking to assess a situation, as well as content knowledge about the Manhattan Project, World War II, the factors that contributed to Japan's involvement in the war, and the bombing of Hiroshima and Nagasaki and the consequences of those events. "In order to really understand how much a student knows, or doesn't know, we may need to go beyond the student's first response and dig deeper" (Cooper 2011, 112). Ask probing questions that require the student to dig deeper.

As we develop questions to assess student learning, we need to attend to the type and level of questions we ask. The learning goals we are assessing dictate the type of questions we ask. They also determine the degree to which we are assessing the depth or breadth of the students' understanding of the content. For immediate feedback as to the students' knowledge of factual information, closed-ended questions are appropriate. Closed-ended questions have only one correct answer. Open-ended questions have more than one correct answer and usually require a degree of critical thinking. So they are more appropriate when you want to evaluate students' in-depth understanding of the content and its application.

The level of questions asked can vary, depending on whether we are assessing lower or higher levels of critical thinking. Lower-order, knowledge-level questions are "what" questions, which test a student's ability to recall information. Higher-order questions address the "how" and "why." These questions are designed to test the students' critical thinking skills. Bloom (1956) identified six levels of higher-order thinking: knowledge, comprehension, application, analysis, synthesis, and evaluation.

Knowledge-level questions focus on specific facts and information and have a clear response. Comprehension questions require students to be able to explain a construct and provide examples of the concept. Application-level questions require students to use the knowledge they have learned to solve problems or address situations or issues. Analysis-level questions require the learner to break down information into parts, examining elements, relationships, or organization. Synthesis questions require students to compile information from various sources or concepts to address an issue. Finally, evaluation-level questions require learners to make judgments about information, defending their position with evidence.

Ultimately, the questions we choose should help students think more deeply about the content and their own reasoning. To encourage deep thinking, we should consider using questions to assess more than the students' cognitive skills. We can also use questions to assess the affective domain, working with students to consider their attitudes and emotional connection to the content. Questions of the affective domain will focus on the value that students place on what they learned and how it impacts their personal behavior and attitudes.

Also consider alternative ways of responding to questions beyond verbal or written responses. As we design questions, we need to consider our purpose. Determine if you need to assess the students' ability to craft a verbal or written response, or whether you want to assess their content knowledge. Some students are better able to respond verbally or in writing, while others may understand the content and be able to answer the question but do not have the skills to express themselves adequately verbally or in writing. Use this as an opportunity to build on the students' other strengths, providing them with opportunities to express their knowledge through drawings or other physical representations of the content.

## QUESTIONING STRATEGIES

Questioning can be used to support formative assessment using a variety of instructional strategies: class discussions, debate, consensus building, and interactive lecture. As you plan the discussion or interactive presentation, avoid ineffective questioning strategies. Involve your students in discussions that go beyond rote-level information. "While estimates vary, studies suggest that between 70 and 95 percent of all teacher questions are the kind of questions that do not require deep thinking" (Sadker, Sadker, and Zittleman 2011, 110).

Assessing students' ability to remember the material they've read or on which they've taken notes has a degree of value. However, knowledge-level questions do not spur in-depth discussion or promote critical thinking. Discussions should serve as a tool to help students apply what they've learned to a new problem or to their own situation, connecting what they've learned to what they already know and thereby enhancing retention of information. This section provides detail on the use of instructional methods that utilize questioning to formatively assess student achievement.

### Discussion

Open discussions with an overarching question designed to capture the attention of the students and engage them in the topic being addressed can be an effective formative assessment tool. Gaining the students' interest at the beginning of the discussion is key to ensuring their participation and hence your ability to assess their learning. The quality of the questions asked, once you have their attention, will determine the quality of the achievement data you obtain.

Discussion serves as a means to assess student learning, while at the same time accelerating learning. Learning is enhanced when we acknowledge the expertise the students bring to class and help them make connections between what they know and what they are learning. Class discussion is an excellent opportunity to help students identify these relationships.

To utilize discussion as a formative assessment tool, it is important that you develop a method for tracking student responses, evaluating the depth and accuracy with which they respond to questions. A log sheet with a simple scoring scheme can be used to track student performance. Label columns with the learning outcomes you will be assessing during the discussion, allowing for two columns per outcome. Use one column to score the depth of the response and the second to assess accuracy. Label the rows with the students' names. The discussion itself must be well planned, as you will be scoring student responses while facilitating the discussion and asking probing questions to gain a better understanding of student learning.

In your planned discussion, incorporate questions that will allow you to ensure your interpretation of the students' understanding. Ask them to provide more information, clarify their response, or provide an example to further illustrate their meaning. Use guiding questions to help them compare and contrast two concepts: "What do they have in common?" or "How are they different?" Help them identify cause and effect: "What happened first?" "What was the result?" "Why?"

Assess the students' ability to paraphrase or summarize what they have learned, rather than their ability to repeat information verbatim. You do not truly understand something until you can explain it simply. Students need to be able to explain the concepts simply, clearly, and succinctly. Strive to help them achieve this level of understanding.

*Debate*

Debate is another effective discussion format that can be used to enhance learning while also assessing students' critical thinking, comprehension, and understanding of the learning objectives. An important element in engaging students in debate is to select an interesting, somewhat controversial, but relevant topic. Debates can be used to foster critical thinking, encouraging students to analyze and research issues and to identify inconsistencies, and to find documentation that supports their position.

Debates also give students a purpose for developing clarity in their explanations and for developing their research, presentation, and public speaking skills. It provides them a meaningful opportunity to organize their thoughts and develop persuasive arguments, and requires them to identify examples and documentation to support their position.

Debates can be organized as class debates or as debates to be conducted between small groups or individuals. As a cooperative learning activity (Hopkins 2013), students can be organized into teams of five. Each team member would be assigned a role to play within the debate:

- Lead—presents the main points of the argument developed by the team
- Questioner—poses questions about the argument presented by the opposing team to the team member who will be responding to the opposing team's argument
- Responder—takes over the role of Lead, responding to the opposition's argument by answering the questions posed by the questioner
- Rebutter—replies to the opposition's responder, and the new arguments raised by the opposition's response
- Summarizer—closes the debate, summarizing the team's main points and their arguments against the opposition's efforts to break down their argument

In preparing for the debate, students work together collaboratively to develop their arguments. Each team member takes on a specific role within the debate. The organization of the roles described above requires each team member to be equally prepared for the debate and to have a clear understanding of the content and issues they are addressing. Each team provides opening, closing, and summary arguments, unlike in competitive debate.

To conduct the debate, the teacher or a student not participating in the current debate serves as moderator, introducing the debaters in their individual roles and posing the question or issue being debated. To reduce classroom management issues, the debate needs to be monitored, adhering to relatively strict time frames, so that the debate does not drag on and reduce student engagement. The moderator ensures that the debate follows a clear, regulated format:

> The lead for the Affirmative team presents the main points of the team's argument supporting the issue being debated (6–10 minutes).
>
> The Negative team works to punch holes in the Affirmative team's argument by having the Negative team's questioner cross-examine their team responder (3–5 minutes).
>
> The lead for the Negative team presents the main points of their team's argument against the issue being debated (6–10 minutes).
>
> The Negative team then conducts a cross-examination, with their questioner asking questions that are designed to punch holes in the Affirmative team's argument, of the Negative team's responder (3–5 minutes).
>
> The rebutter for the Affirmative team responds (3–5 minutes).
>
> The rebutter for the Negative team responds (3–5 minutes).

The summarizer for the Affirmative team summarizes the team's main points and reinforces the arguments brought to bear during their team's cross-examination (6–10 minutes).

The summarizer for the Negative team summarizes the team's main points and reinforces the arguments brought to bear during their team's cross-examination (6–10 minutes).

To actively engage the class members who are observing the debate, have them judge the debate by having students keep a running tally of new points introduced by each team during the course of the debate. Conclude the debate by engaging the class in a discussion about the debate, examining the critical points made by each team and the effectiveness of their arguments. In the end, have the students determine which side of the debate presented the stronger case.

To use the debate as a formative assessment tool, you will evaluate each team's arguments and the comprehension each team member demonstrated related to those arguments. Given the roles assigned to each team member, they will each have the opportunity and need to demonstrate their knowledge of the issue and the arguments presented by their team. Prior to assessing the debate, however, identify the key learning outcomes you want to focus on. Develop a scoring rubric related to those skills and constructs, and use that rubric to score not only the team preparation, but also the degree to which each team member demonstrated the learning outcomes you have identified.

## Consensus Building

Consensus building or collaborative problem solving is a team process that involves the students in conflict resolution (Consensus Research Consortium 1998). To be an effective and engaging learning activity and a valuable formative assessment tool, it is important that the issue being discussed is one without apparent consensus that the students see as being relevant and meaningful.

This activity can be carried out as a class activity or by teams of four or five students. Each participant should bring varied views and individual expertise related to the topic of discussion or the problem to be addressed. Students will bring their knowledge of the content, critical thinking strategies, and personal beliefs to the consensus building process, and each point in the process provides the teacher with the opportunity to observe and assess student learning in both the cognitive and affective domains.

The first step in the process is defining the problem or issue to be addressed. For example, in a health class you might complete a conflict resolution activity by having the students consider the incidence of teen pregnancy and sexually active teens in their school, district, or state. The students might clarify the issue, choosing to address questions such as

"Should the high school nurse's office provide birth control to students? If so, what forms of birth control should be provided? Should the emphasis be on abstinence or on safe sex? What is the school's responsibility in terms of teaching students about safe sex?"

The group will then brainstorm alternative approaches to addressing the issue. Then, if you are conducting this as a whole class activity, divide the students into teams to research the issue and the approaches that were brainstormed. Each team would tackle different issues or aspects related to the overall problem. Given the example just presented, students might research the incidence of teen pregnancy, implications and issues related to the use of different forms of birth control, the impact of similar programs on the incidence of teen pregnancy, community views on the issues, and consequences of unprotected sexual activity.

Students would bring their research back to the group and share their findings. As they work together, students should be encouraged to work toward "mutually advantageous approaches." Alternatives are identified, and the perceived costs, benefits, and barriers to each approach are discussed. Eventually, the choice is narrowed down to one approach. This approach is fine-tuned until all the students agree with the proposed solution.

Consensus building is a wonderful opportunity to observe student thinking and their understanding of the content, even if a common solution is never identified. An activity such as this provides a means to engage students in critical thinking and in the process of looking at all sides of an issue. It also provides a means to examine the ability of students to use persuasive argument in their attempt to convince other students to support their viewpoint.

In using consensus building as a tool to formatively assess student learning, it is important to identify the objectives you wish to assess through the activity. Develop a log and rubric to track and evaluate student performance throughout the entire activity. Consider key points at which you can provide student feedback designed to help individual students improve their performance. Activities such as this provide us with an excellent opportunity to not only assess learning but also actively improve student performance as the activity proceeds.

## INTERACTIVE LECTURE

When you are delivering a presentation or lecture to students, questions are generally limited to a one-on-one interaction between the teacher and one student. The student who is formatively assessed is the one who chooses to answer the question. Technology has revolutionized the questioning process with personal response systems, commonly called clickers. During a presentation, a question can be posed and all the students respond to the question using a small device similar to a remote. You will immediately know the percentage of students who responded correctly and understand the concept the question was designed to address.

This allows the teacher to efficiently and effectively gather data on student achievement and understanding. If the technology is unavailable, teachers may give students small whiteboards on which to write their responses, and then visually check the accuracy of the student response. With either system, you use the data immediately to change or improve instruction. This is an opportunity for you to reinforce or reteach the concepts being taught.

As we integrate questions into lecture and presentations, it is important to consider both the type of questions we ask and the timing of questions. The timing of questions can help students process their learning, as well as provide us information about their understanding of the concepts being taught.

We can select, construct, and time questions so that they have the greatest impact on student thinking and on the eventual application of the constructs being taught. As stated previously, ask questions that go beyond rote level. Ask questions that require students to think critically about the content and how it relates to their prior knowledge. Given that a clicker system has the appearance of being anonymous, it may also be a good tool for assessing learning outcomes in the affective domain. If students perceive the assessment to be anonymous, they are more likely to answer questions truthfully.

## IMPLEMENTATION

Discussion is a tool that can be easily implemented throughout the learning process. It can be used at the beginning of a lesson to assess students' prior knowledge and at any point during instruction to refine the teaching strategies being implemented. Log sheets and rubrics aligned to the learning outcomes being assessed during the discussion should be developed at the time you design the learning activity. Overall, it's a good idea to keep the rubric simple, with only two to three levels of performance. This will allow you to score individual student performance quickly and efficiently.

When using discussion as a measure of learning, you will need to be able to perform multiple tasks at the same time. You will be facilitating and monitoring the discussion, looking for opportunities to ask additional questions or a probing question to help the students delve with greater depth or breadth into the issue being discussed. You will also need to be attentive to student behavior and participation. Classroom management is an ongoing issue that will always require a portion of your attention. Therefore, to ensure the reliability of discussion as a formative assessment measure, the tools you use to score the assessment need to be clear, specific, and easy to use.

## CONCLUSION

Second only to lecture, discussion is one of the most common instructional strategies implemented in the classroom. When used skillfully, questions can be used to engage students and to gain a greater understanding of the depth and breadth of their content knowledge. The teacher's questioning skills and the quality of the questions they ask determine the degree to which those questions foster learning. The quality of questions asked and the alignment of those questions with the learning goals they are designed to assess also determine the reliability and validity of their use as a measure of student learning.

Questions and discussion that are easily integrated into instruction and into activities designed to engage students with the content can be used to assess not only the students' content knowledge but also their ability to implement critical thinking. In this chapter we have discussed the use of discussion and a variety of teaching strategies utilizing discussion to support learning and the formative assessment process.

To implement discussion as a formative assessment measure, you must identify and design questions that align directly with the learning outcomes you want to assess, prior to instruction. You need to follow the same guidelines when you develop rubrics that are used to score student responses and their performance in discussion situations such as debate and consensus-building activities. With well-designed questions and issues to foster discussion among the students about the content, learning activities such as discussion, debate, consensus building, and interactive lecture can be used to inform instruction and support student learning.

# TWELVE

## Technology

As the world has become more technology-driven, a number of tools have become available that support real-time data collection during the teaching and learning process. In this chapter we will explore a variety of technologies that can easily be implemented in the classroom setting, including clickers, smart boards, tablets, and cell phones.

Technology can support any stage within a well-defined assessment process. Technology can help teachers track and monitor student progress, and adaptive testing software can allow us to tailor assessments to individual students. Technology tools including computers, personal response systems, and mobile devices can be used to deliver assessments. Mobile devices and computer software can be used to track, score, and interpret findings. These devices can also be used to provide audio, video, and text-based feedback. To be usable as a formative assessment tool, the technology must be easy to use, dependable, and accurate.

Depending on the application ("app"), software program, mobile technology, or other hardware we choose to use, a number of features can be at our finger tips. These tools can be flexible, allowing us to adjust parameters and choose when and where the tool is used. Technology tools can be used to record group processes and document student work electronically. Online or computer-based assessments can be scored by the computer using the protocol you have set up.

Learning management systems (LMS) and computer-based assessments can easily grade multiple choice or short response assessments. Many technologies allow for quick review of student responses. What is especially nice is that the systems can be used to provide students with immediate feedback. Support and feedback can be rapidly disseminated to the students in online learning environments. Within the system, you can store and analyze data electronically.

Automated text-comparison services such as Turnitin can be used to detect plagiarism and provide feedback to students on their paraphrasing and citation skills. You can also take advantage of the technology's capability to enhance accessibility. If students are dyslexic or blind, technology can be used to provide audio support. A screen reader can be used to read text and assessment questions to students. The image size on a computer screen can also be adjusted for size and contrast for students who have visual issues.

## USING TECHNOLOGY FOR EASY RECORD KEEPING

One of the greatest benefits of using technology to support the formative process is that you can easily and efficiently record and track student data. Many applications ("apps") designed for use on mobile devices such as smart phones or tablets come with recording systems built in; data is tracked and recorded automatically as the assessment is completed.

You can also build your own recording system in a spreadsheet program, modifying it to fit your unique needs. If you are also recording data in an online program or application, there is the distinct possibility you will be able to import the information directly to your spreadsheet. This is great because you don't need to re-record student assessment data into your spreadsheet so that you can have a master record of student performance.

Using a spreadsheet to support your formative assessment process helps you easily retain and store individual and group student data over a period of time. Once data is imported or recorded in the system, you will be able to use the program's capabilities to easily analyze data and create charts and graphs to visualize data. You will also be able to track student performance over time, monitoring progress and looking for trends in student learning. More information on using spreadsheets to support data analysis is available in chapter 13, "Efficiency in Data Collection and Analysis."

## TECHNOLOGY TOOLS

Technology can provide us with an effective and efficient tool for supporting the formative assessment process. In this section we will look at a variety of technology tools that can be used to support the formative assessment process, including personal response systems, interactive whiteboards, mobile applications, concept-mapping software, and learning management systems. These tools can be used to develop interactive lectures, create large screen manipulatives, track observational data, and deliver assessments.

*Clickers*

Personal response systems have become increasingly popular, especially when there are a large number of students in a class. The most important asset of these systems is that the system provides immediate feedback to the teacher and the students. When you use a clicker system to support lecture, you automatically make the presentation being delivered interactive. You also have a wonderful opportunity to formatively assess your students' understanding of the presentation. As you deliver a lecture, you will stop at key points that you have placed into the presentation, and ask your students to respond to a question. All systems support multiple choice responses, and others also support short answer responses.

The system collects each of the responses and collates them for you, creating a graph that lets you know instantly the percentage of students who know the correct answer. If a number of students respond incorrectly, you can stop and engage the students in a discussion and reteach the concept immediately.

After class, you can also look at a detailed listing of student responses and determine which students were unable to identify the correct answer for each of the questions included in the presentation. You will also be able to identify specific questions or concepts with which the class as a whole had trouble. This allows you to do a quick analysis of student learning and identify students who need additional support, as well as identify content you need to take the time to reteach to the class as a whole.

*Interactive Whiteboards*

Interactive whiteboards such as SMART Boards, MimioBoards, and Promethean boards serve as a large touchscreen for your computer. Anything on your computer can be manipulated from the front of the classroom, simply by touching the interactive whiteboard. It can be used to manipulate images, save text or graphics drawn on the whiteboard, or interact with Web-based programs or software.

By using an interactive whiteboard, you can save information written on the board during group discussions and brainstorming sessions. This allows you to log the progression of the discussion. You can also use it to have students manipulate graphics on the board to demonstrate their understanding of concepts. Because you can save the files that are created during instruction, you can analyze these files for trends in learning over time.

In an action research study completed by two Australian kindergarten teachers (Preston and Mowbray 2008), students' understanding of concepts and recall of procedures were evaluated using the manipulation of graphics on a SMART Board. Students manipulated images demonstrating the need for food, water, and sun for plants to grow.

These activities allowed English language learners (ELLs) to complete tasks that they would have struggled with if given a pencil/paper text-based assessment. Interactive whiteboards could also be used for students to manipulate elements of a story, demonstrate understanding of processes such as the water cycle, or engage students with an online learning game such as the math games created by Mangahigh (Preston and Mowbray 2008).

## Mobile Technologies

Tablets, smart phones, and other mobile devices provide wonderful tools to track student data, keep running records, document student performance, and record observations. Applications that allow you to track data, record information on the fly, and analyze data have been designed for use with mobile devices.

iTunes (https://itunes.apple.com) and Google Play (https://play.google.com) offer applications that are designed to specifically support the assessment process, which are available for free or at low cost. Applications range from those created by companies who design apps to support their instructional materials (such as myLexia, which is used to track individual progress with the Lexia Reading system) to systems designed to monitor student progress.

Programs like Teacher's Assistant Pro (Apple) and Teacher's Class Behavior Pro (Android) are designed to help teachers track individual student behavior, allowing the teacher to easily attach descriptors of common behaviors to each student's file. Each behavior is time stamped, allowing you to examine trends relevant to activities occurring in class during the time frame the behavior was exhibited. Super Duper Data Tracker (Apple and Android) is a tool for documenting student progress on individual goals. Teachers can track incorrect and correct responses discreetly and efficiently.

Easy Portfolio (Apple and Android) provides a tool to create electronic portfolios of student work using images, audio files, or documents, stored electronically, chronologically documenting student growth. Easy Rubric (Apple) and Grade Rubric (Android) are applications that can be used to design rubrics and then use the rubric to assess student work. Data can be captured for each individual student and then collated for analysis. AndroClass – Teacher (Android) provides a detailed tool that can be used to track student grades, performance, and behavior. Assist (Apple) takes data analysis a step further. It allows you to track student data and scan bubble sheets, scoring student work quickly.

Other applications have been designed to actually assess student performance on the fly, during class presentations and discussions. Excelegrade (Apple) and Nearpod (Apple) are tools that can be used to give multiple choice or free response assessments to students. These apps allow you to use your iPod or iPad as a personal response system working much the same as clickers do. Students complete the assessment on their mobile device, and responses are collated for the teacher's analysis. Socrative (Android) is a comparable application, but just a little more limited. It can only be used for tracking multiple choice responses from mobile devices.

More specialized applications can be used to provide students with customized formative feedback quickly. Formative Feedback (Apple) is an app that can be used to videotape a student's performance and then annotate the video, commenting on the student's performance and using icons and basic editing tools to provide feedback. Essay Grader (Apple) provides an application that allows you to create a feedback document for each essay you grade. As you grade you select prewritten comments in the areas of praise, organization, content, mechanics, style, and documentation.

Applications are also available to provide written and audio feedback. With Replay Notes (Apple), text and audio are recorded and used to create a YouTube video to share with students. Your mobile devices can also be used to digitally record audio of your assessment feedback. Recording feedback as you score student work allows you to provide immediate feedback to your students without taking time to transcribe your comments. This can also serve as a tool to engage your students in conversation, providing additional opportunities to evaluate student learning.

### Concept-Mapping Software

Concept mapping software can be used to examine how students understand the relationships between concepts. Using programs such as Inspiration or Kidspiration, students can quickly and easily create concept maps that organize the concepts and related indicators. For example, in a reading or literature class students might create a concept map that shows the relationship between characters in the novel *1984* by George Orwell. Students could also correlate parts of the story with current events in the political and medical arenas. This would allow you to observe their understanding of the relationships and their ability to correlate their reading to current events.

### Learning Management Systems

Learning management systems (LMSs) can make it easier to administer assessment tasks, as well as to monitor and track student data. LMSs and other dedicated assessment software programs provide quiz tools that can quickly and easily score multiple choice assessments. Electronic rubrics built into an LMS allow you to quickly score student work. The grade book within the LMS allows you to easily record scores and share those scores with students. LMSs also allow you to move assessment outside of the classroom. Students can complete assessment activities or quizzes outside of class and post them within the LMS, giving the students greater responsibility for their learning.

## IMPLEMENTATION

Technology should not be used just for the sake of using technology. The use needs to be purposeful and should enhance student learning. When using technology in any teaching situation, it's important that the technology be there for a specific purpose. As we determine what technologies to use and when to use them, we need to be mindful of the characteristics of the technology that will most benefit our assessment needs.

When using technology as part of the formative assessment process, we need to clearly communicate the assessment requirements to students. If we are expecting students to complete formative assessments outside of class, this is even more important. You will not be there for students to ask you questions, so the assessment tools need to be easy to access and use.

If you are using an LMS to administer quizzes, students need to be given specific directions on how to access and use the system. Online quizzes need to be configured so as to give students adequate time to complete the quiz, but not so much time that they can use outside resources to find the answers (unless that is the intent). Directions for performance assessments also need to be clear, outlining specifically how to complete the task and expectations for their performance.

Using clickers or smart phone apps as personal response systems during instruction not only provides us valuable tools for formatively assessing student understanding of the lesson, but also is a means to increase student interaction. During a longer lecture or presentation a sequence of questions should be planned for every ten to fifteen minutes, breaking up the presentation into smaller learning segments. Shifting the level and type of student activity will allow them to concentrate better and remain engaged in the presentation.

Make sure questions are clear, grammatically correct, and support the concept you are trying to assess. Be sure to stagger the questions throughout your presentation at key intervals. Do not place all questions at the end of the lecture, causing you to rush the presentation so that you have enough time for the assessment. By designing questions that focus on the most important points of the lecture and inserting them into the presentation in close relation to the topic, you are able to reinforce those concepts that are most critical for student learning.

When assessing students individually or in small groups using an interactive whiteboard or other tool, you need to have designed learning activities that will keep students occupied while they are waiting to be assessed. The learning activities need to require limited attention from you. Your attention should be on the student(s)' completing the assessment. Keep noisy activities farther away from the area in which you are conducting the assessment.

For formative assessment purposes keep your assessments short, so that you can move quickly as you assess each student, and keep the assessment focused. If possible, schedule a teaching assistant, paraprofessional, or parent volunteer to work with students who are waiting to be assessed. Develop small group activities in which students can support one another at learning centers while you are completing individualized assessment. Make sure the centers are well supplied with the necessary materials, and make sure the students understand the rules and routines so that they can work independently.

Using online tools to support assessment will also give students more responsibility for their learning. To foster individual responsibility for learning we need to first be clear with our expectations. We also need to build an environment that encourages active learning. We need to be prepared for class, creating interactive lessons that make appropriate use of the technologies and other resources we use to facilitate instruction and assessment.

We need to break instruction and assessment into palatable chunks, giving students time to process information and make connections. Finally, we need to provide students the tools that allow them to take responsibility and control of their own learning. Help students understand the relevance of the curriculum, and align your assessment practices to the learning objectives. Allow students to track their own progress, give them access to assessment data, and help them understand the meaning of their individual scores. Help them make learning goals, and give them the tools to reach those goals.

## CONCLUSION

One of the greatest benefits to using technology to support assessment is the fact that feedback can be immediate. As you choose technology tools to support formative assessment, look for tools that will help you easily share assessment results and feedback with students and parents. Learning requires frequent feedback, as well as practice and opportunities to apply knowledge.

Learning also involves the ability of students to monitor their own learning. For students to monitor their own learning, we must provide specific, context-dependent feedback that will allow them to improve their performance. Technology can help us do this to a certain degree, but we need to add the critical elements to that technology. We can use the tools to let students know where they are in terms of performance. We need to challenge and engage students, giving them the feedback that will help them make connections. Technology is one of the tools we can use to do that.

Using technology to support the formative assessment process gives you the ability to leverage the data you are collecting to assign a grade or address external accountability requirements. We will be able to use this data more efficiently to support data-informed decision making. Data can be used to examine student performance and also to share information about individual student progress with students and their parents.

Technology also makes it easier to personalize our assessments and therefore instruction. These tools can allow you to track individual student performance, identify strengths, weaknesses, and opportunities to intervene, and thereby better support student learning. In the end, the success of any technology tool is dependent upon usability of data obtained to support and enhance student learning. Quality of data is far more important than quantity. Technology tools should be used to collect quality data that provides us a clear picture of student performance on specific learning objectives.

# THIRTEEN

# Efficiency in Data Collection and Analysis

Formative assessment has limited value if data is not easily gathered, disaggregated, and analyzed. In this chapter we will discuss methods for efficiently gathering and recording the results from formative assessments. Techniques for disaggregating and analyzing the data will also be discussed, with instructions in the use of various technologies that support this process.

Unfortunately, for many of us formative assessment stops with the grading of the assessment. To have an impact on teaching and learning, we need to make the formative assessment process usable. To be usable, the data must be easily gathered, recorded in a format that can be quickly analyzed, and provide meaningful information that can be used to inform instruction and the learning process.

The formative assessment system, most importantly, needs to reflect the tasks the teacher wants to accomplish with the data. In designing your formative assessment system, consider how the system can be used to meet the various needs you will find in the classroom. You need to be able to locate and retrieve data that is relevant to the instructional situation and students' needs. Foremost, the data has to be usable and productive.

## DATA COLLECTION

Gathering assessment data is not enough; we must analyze the data and apply what we learn to our instruction. After determining the student data we want to monitor and collect, we need to determine the format for recording student performance on those key learning objectives. It can be useful to create a data collection template using a table, grid, or spreadsheet. Organize data according to the standard and the indicator that is being assessed.

Consider how frequently you want to collect data. Since the purpose of data collection is to inform instruction and learning, data regarding student performance should be collected at least every two weeks. Depending on the learning goal being monitored and the amount of instructional time dedicated to teaching the goal, it may be appropriate to track performance on a daily basis.

Based upon the data collected, you will want to address a number of key questions (Maryland State Department of Education 2012):

- What percentage of students demonstrated proficiency?
- What implications does that have for instruction?
- Which students have not demonstrated that they can do this?
- Based on individual student performance, what do I need to do next to move the students to proficiency?
- Based on the class performance, what reteaching do I need to do?

Remember, this is a cyclical process, so it's important to follow up on specific data points and consider the following questions:

- After reassessing, did my students demonstrate proficiency?
- Is my reteaching or other intervention resulting in improved student performance?
- When we compare performance by subgroups (e.g., by racial group, gender, students with disabilities, ESL students, or students in the free and reduced meals program), do we see any groups not performing as well as the whole group? If so, what are we going to do about that?
- Do we have any students who are not attaining proficiency across indicators?
- What interventions have I tried? What interventions do I plan to try next?

As you consider these questions, you will want to reflect on the teaching and learning process and determine those concepts that need to be retaught using different methods or materials. You will want to identify specific methods that are ineffective and methods that have helped students learn concepts most efficiently.

## DATA COLLECTION TOOLS

As you gather data regarding student performance, it is important that you have a clear understanding of the learning outcomes you are assessing and what good student work looks like. You also need to be able to record detailed observation notes regarding student performance. Additionally, you may want to record your own thoughts on student work and your interpretation of that work. Doing these activities will allow you to generate quality data that you can use to assess student achievement overall.

As you review student work that does not indicate proficiency, you will want to be able to make detailed notes about their performance that you can then use to guide instruction. As you evaluate each student's performance on a given formative assessment, you'll want to identify what the student is able to do correctly, as well as misconceptions or incorrect information that he or she demonstrates.

You will also need to note learning outcomes that a student did not demonstrate in the assessment that he or she should have demonstrated. If a student does not demonstrate specific skills, we need to consider other methods we could use to find out if the student really did not know the information. It is possible that the student could have demonstrated the skill but chose not to do so. We need to not just assume the student does not have the skill just because he or she does not demonstrate it in a particular assessment.

*Rubrics*

Rubrics are a valuable tool for assessing performance or authentic assessments that are being used as formative assessments. These can be used to evaluate writing activities such as free-writes, observations, and discussions, as well as other performance assessments. When designed with well-detailed performance indicators, rubrics have the potential to support learning and improve instruction (Jonsson and Svingby 2007). Rubrics make expectations and criteria clear to the student, supporting self-assessment by the student. They also provide a ready and easy tool for you to use in scoring formative assessments. Rubrics allow you to quickly and easily provide constructive feedback to individual students.

For formative assessments, develop rubrics that focus directly on the learning outcomes the assessment is designed to evaluate, rather than on the mechanics of the activity. Consider focusing the assessment on only one or two learning outcomes. Identify the characteristics you want the students to demonstrate through the assessment. Focus on those characteristics that will tell you what the student can do in terms of the learning outcome.

We should pay specific attention to the identified learning outcomes, or those indicators that will help scaffold the learner in their development toward meeting the objective. Remember to focus on those learning outcomes that are key to student success with the content, rather on those that could be classified as "nice to know" but not essential. Identify specific categories that can be used to assess the student's ability as it relates to each learning outcome. Keep the categories clear and distinct, so that the assessment of each can be used to provide useful information related to student performance.

Define a minimum of two performance levels for each category, providing a clear behavioral description that details the expectations required to achieve each level. Reliability is higher with fewer levels. However, include enough levels so that the assessment will provide you with specific information about each student's ability to complete the assigned task. Do not have more levels than you can define. Avoid using ranges, unless you can clearly describe differences within the range. To use a scoring range of 8–10, you would need to be able to describe the difference between a score of 8, 9, and 10. Consider the example in figure 13.1.

As you identify the criteria you will use to assess student work, consider using specific indicators associated directly with the learning goal. This will improve inter-rater and intra-rater reliability. Criteria should be

**CCSS Speaking and Listening, Grade 5, Standard 3:** Summarize the points a speaker makes and explain how each claim is supported by reasons.

**Task:** After a presentation made by a guest speaker or teacher, students will complete a timed writing activity. Students must identify one point that the speaker made and cite two reasons provided by the speaker which verifies the point.

Categories:

Narrative summary of key points
Identifies specific points
Supports each point identified

Performance Levels:

Mastery
Developing
Needs Work

Rubric:

| | Mastery | Developing | Needs Work |
|---|---|---|---|
| Narrative summary of key points | Main idea clearly stated with supportive details included with good detail. | Main idea stated with supportive details. | Main idea not clear or not supported. |
| Identifies specific points | One point made by the speaker is clearly identified. | One point is identified but it is not clearly defined. | An attempt is made to identify one or more points made by the speaker. |
| Supports each point identified | Two or more reasons provided which clearly support the point identified. | One or more reasons are provided which seem to support the point identified. | An attempt is made to support a point made by the speaker, but association is not clear or is inaccurate. |

**Figure 13.1.   Rubric example**

chosen with care, making sure that they support the learning objectives being assessed by the rubric. Use the rubric to provide specific feedback to students. Take the time to provide specific feedback for each criterion, so the students can use the feedback to improve their performance.

Rubrics that are designed for use with a specific activity are more likely to produce generalizable and dependable scores than generic rubrics designed for use with multiple activities (Jonsson and Svingby 2007). The more complex a rubric is, with multiple levels, the more difficult it is to use consistently. Keep criteria clear and use the minimal number of performance levels that will provide you with the information you need to make instructional decisions. This will provide you with more reliable feedback on student performance and make the formative assessment process more efficient.

### Checklists

Checklists are essentially simple rubrics designed with a two- or possibly three-point rating scale. They are useful when a simple yes/no, proficient/not proficient, or novice/intermediate/proficient evaluation of the performance is appropriate. Points may or may not be associated with each rating. An assessment checklist takes each indicator associated with the learning goal and turns it into a statement that describes the behavior. For example, with a writing assignment, statements might read as follows: "Student uses periods appropriately" or "Student has a clear main idea for each paragraph."

Designing a checklist begins by first identifying a performance activity based on the learning objectives you want to address. Once a task has been identified, you need to outline your expectations in clear detail. It's important that you give students a complete understanding of your expectations as to the task and what behaviors you are specifically looking for. Next, determine the dimensions of the performance activity you will be evaluating, writing specific behavioral statements that describe the performance you should observe.

If you are assessing an insect collection, you might evaluate the student's ability to identify the genus and species, organize insects into their correct genus, and the "correct use of domain specific words and phrases" (CCSS.ELA-Literacy.RST.6-8.4). One of your behavioral statements might read: "Student correctly identifies scientific name, genus and species." Finally, we would assign points or descriptive terms to each rating, such as yes/no, proficient/not proficient or novice/intermediate/proficient to each descriptor.

A simply designed checklist makes a good data collection template that is quick and easy to use to evaluate student skills. It can be used by the teacher to monitor student performance or gather observation data quickly or by students to self-evaluate. The checklist can be used by students to ensure that they have completed all of the steps or considered all of the possibilities in completing a task. They are also excellent tools for differentiating instruction for students who have difficulty completing a process-based task, providing them with a step-by-step guide to complete the task.

## Grade Book

If designed appropriately, a grade book can be used as an excellent tool for tracking student progress. To do so, it must be aligned with the standards and learning outcomes associated with the class. Each standard can become a category within the grade book, and within each category each indicator associated with the standard should be identified. The categories would then be used to organize the grade book.

The grade book can serve as a good data collection template if it is aligned with the indicators that are aligned with the content standards or learning outcomes. You could color code the data in the grade book according to how you have defined student performance (e.g., nearing proficiency, proficient, and advanced). By color coding each level of proficiency, such as coloring scores that indicate nearing proficiency as red, proficient as yellow, and advanced as green, you will be able to quickly identify students at varying levels of proficiency. A system such as this will allow you to quickly identify those who need additional support or those who need to be challenged to a greater extent.

## Student Data Books

To enhance student learning, it is effective to teach students how to monitor their own achievement data. We can help students set long-term and short-term learning goals based on their individual performance data. Then we need to work with students to reach educational goals (National Center for Education Evaluation and Regional Assistance 2009). Too frequently students think that teachers "give scores." They don't realize that they actually earn their scores. Many do not understand the impact of their own efforts on the grades they earn.

By helping students understand the meaning of the learning objectives and their own performance data, we can help them take control of their own learning. To this end, data presented in a manner that is easily understood, descriptive, and accessible to students can help them understand their own academic strengths and weaknesses.

To appropriately implement student data books, you must first explain your expectations and assessment criteria to your students. This needs to be done for each unit of instruction, assisting students to understand where their performance fits as defined by the expectations and assessment data. We should work with the students to develop a data book in which they can track their own scores from formative, summative, and short-cycle assessments.

The scores need to be associated with the learning goals they are designed to assess. Scores from assessments using the same scale can be compared, showing the growth in the student's skills. In addition to data, we need to provide students with feedback that is timely, specific, and constructive. Feedback should help students understand their strengths and weaknesses and give them direction as to how to improve their own performance.

Finally, we need to provide students with tools that will help them learn from assessment data and feedback. Time should be set aside in class for students to interpret, learn from, and reflect on their own progress. During this time, we can have students review and reflect on the feedback and then ask questions about the feedback. To support this we should develop templates for the students to list their strengths, weaknesses, and areas on which the student should focus for a given task (see table 13.1).

**Table 13.1.   Example of a Student's Data Reflection Worksheet**

**Areas of Strength and Areas of Growth**

**Topic:** Demonstrate command of the conventions of standard English grammar and usage when writing or speaking.
a. Use parallel structure.*
b. Use various types of phrases (noun, verb, adjectival, adverbial, participial, prepositional, absolute) and clauses (independent, dependent; noun, relative, adverbial) to convey specific meanings and add variety and interest to writing or presentations.
(CCSS, Language Standards 6-12, Standard 1)
**Data Source:** Rubric score and written feedback on one minute essays, journals, and chapter essay responses
**Name:** Margaret Espinoza

Areas of Strength

Grammar and Usage
Appropriate punctuation
Correctly capitalize sentences

Parallel Structure:
Consistent grammatical form within sentences
Keeps correlative conjunctions parallel

Variety in Phrasing:
Focuses on simple sentences that are phrased correctly

Students need to be encouraged to challenge themselves, striving to beat their own highest score. We can have them identify, for themselves, skills they will focus on over the next few lessons. Students can be allowed to correct assessment items that they answered incorrectly, allowing them to learn what is required and increasing their skill in those specific areas. We can provide graphs that track student progress over time and create grids for students to record baseline and formative scores to track gains in mastering learning outcomes.

When we involve students in data analysis, they can become motivated learners, continually reaching for higher goals. They can be further motivated when they map out goals that are attainable and meaningful. It gives students a sense of control over their own learning outcomes when they understand the assessment data that describes their capabilities.

In turn, teachers can use the goals that students set to understand student motivators and use this information to adjust their instruction accordingly. You can review work and assessments students have corrected to identify objectives that need to be retaught. Additionally, students can be grouped by their learning goals or self-identified weaknesses. You can then provide instruction to address those goals or weaknesses. You can also design whole class instruction to address common problems.

## DISAGGREGATING AND ANALYZING DATA

Once data is collected, it's important to take the time to analyze data looking at individual students as well as from a whole group perspective. We should look beyond the performance of the class as a whole to how individual students are doing in terms of meeting the learning objectives. We also need to look for trends within the results. To do this, you will need to look beyond individual and whole class performance. Student data should be disaggregated based upon a variety of factors, including ethnicity, gender, and eligibility for free and reduced lunch. We need to look for inequities and consider whether those inequities have been propagated through instructional or assessment procedures, methods, or materials that have been utilized for instruction.

When possible, make graphs of student data. A visual representation of the data will allow you to more easily and quickly analyze the data and draw relevant conclusions. The graph format you use depends on the information you are looking for. In reviewing individual data, make use of line graphs, in which you can easily see individual student performance and progress.

Bar graphs are useful when you are looking for differences in performance between groups of students. Beyond disaggregating scores based upon the demographics previously mentioned (ethnicity, gender, and SES), consider examining differences based upon previous performance. Compare student scores across ability levels: low, medium, and high.

This will allow you to identify trends in students' performance at a certain level and determine if the learning needs of these students are being addressed.

A box-and-whiskers plot is a graph that shows not only the central tendency of the student data but also the range of the data. The box-and-whiskers plot clearly delineates low and high scores, the median score, and the first through third quartiles. It works well in reviewing data collected over time, such as you would have if you were tracking student progress on a specific outcome over time. By averaging scores from each assessment, you could see how the class as a whole has progressed. This type of graph allows you to see growth for low-, medium-, and high-performing students.

*Using Excel and Other Spreadsheets as a Data Analysis Tool*

Spreadsheet programs such as Excel can be used to analyze data and create graphs that display the data. Excel can be used to easily determine the descriptive statistics for a data set, including range, mean, median, mode, and standard deviation. If you would like to be more adventurous while looking at student performance statistically, Excel can also be used to complete t-tests. The findings from a t-test can be used to calculate the statistical importance of a specific score. You might use a t-test to determine if a student's achievement gains are significantly different based upon a specific instructional intervention you have implemented rather than just happenstance.

Excel comes with an "add-in," Data Analysis—Descriptive Statistics, which will provide you with a complete listing of the descriptive statistics associated with a particular data set. Individual formulas can also be used to determine average (mean), median (middle score), and mode (most frequent score). Formulas can also be used to determine the range (high and low values) and standard deviation (how distributed are the scores). Excel also easily creates line and bar graphs. It is possible to create a box-and-whiskers plot in Excel, but it is difficult.

## FEEDBACK

Feedback is a key element of the formative assessment process, but it is easy to overlook. We need to remember that formative assessment should be a collaboration between the teacher and students. If we provide feedback to our students, we give them the opportunity to play an active role in helping to improve their own performance. If students don't know what they are doing wrong (or right), they will be unable to change their performance. Clear, specific feedback needs to be given to students so that they can use this information to modify their performance or personal learning strategies.

Feedback allows you to identify the gap between the level at which the student is currently working and the level at which he or she needs to be in relation to the learning goal. When the learning issue relates to faulty interpretation of the requirements of an assignment, provide corrective feedback that includes specific information about the accuracy of the work. Feedback should be used to identify areas where the student needs to delve more deeply into the content and provide more information or depth in his or her responses.

For more complex learning tasks, in which the students demonstrate a lack of understanding of the underlying processes of a specific task, feedback that focuses on improving error detection is appropriate. Additional feedback can be used to teach students about cuing strategies that can be used to help them follow process guidelines.

Students will be able to develop their own self-assessment skills when we use feedback to teach them how to regulate their own learning. Students can be taught how to evaluate their own work, as well as how to process feedback from other sources. This will help students learn to seek feedback rather than avoid it, and it will help them want to use it to improve their performance. By teaching students how to self-assess, we can increase their confidence in their own abilities and the quality of their work.

Feedback can also be used by students to revise work. We can also make use of peer feedback, in which students learn the content in greater depth through the process of evaluating their classmates' work. This peer feedback can in turn be used by students to revise their work before submitting it for a grade. The important thing is to provide descriptive feedback that is focused on the task and the learning goal rather than on the individual, all done in a timely manner. The feedback we give should help students close the gap between the learning goal and their current performance.

## MAINTAINING EFFICIENCY

Of key importance throughout the formative assessment process is to maintain efficiency. If the data collection and analysis process becomes too cumbersome, it may become too difficult to continue. To maintain efficiency, keep assessments quick and simple. Do not design elaborate assessments intended to assess multiple learning outcomes. Focus on assessing one or two learning goals at a time. Develop evaluation schemes that are clear and quick to implement. Make use of checklists or simple rubrics to assess performance assessments. Make use of technology tools such as student response systems to record multiple choice items.

Use a template to record student data, if possible, at the time of the assessment. If you cannot record data immediately, try to record scores on the day of the assessment. Use visual cues whenever possible, highlighting low or high scores within a data set and diagnosing weaknesses as you record scores. As we review student data, we should pinpoint specific weaknesses of students who are not performing as expected.

After analyzing the data, group together those students with similar instructional needs. We should identify group goals for the students in each group and then plan instruction that will help students meet those goals. Grouping students will allow you to implement an instructional plan for students in small, homogenous groups.

Rather than designing individual learning plans for twenty to thirty students, you will be able to design lessons for two or three groups. You will then need to monitor the students' progress in achieving the goals, adjusting instruction and reorganizing groups as needed. It is essential that you allow the groups to be flexible, adjusting them to meet student needs as they learn and grow and based upon their skill with the current content.

## CONCLUSION

When implementing a formative assessment process, achievement gains are maximized when

1. assessments provide accurate data regarding student performance
2. students are provided frequent descriptive and informative feedback
3. students are involved in the assessment process, through record keeping and communication of findings (Black and Wiliam 1998b)

Learning is maximized when assessment is utilized to support the teaching and learning process.

If not watched closely, formative assessment can become cumbersome. At key points during the school year, step back and look at the assessment protocol you've implemented. Consider: How did the class do as a whole? Which students made significant progress? How? Which students made little or no progress? Why? What is the outlook for the rest of the school year and on into next year? Were they able to achieve a year's growth? What about catch-up growth? Has the gap been narrowed from where they are to where they need to be?

We need to continually track student growth and our own ability to improve student learning. Formative assessment should be used as a tool to improve not only student learning but also our own ability to impact that learning. This chapter has provided you with a number of tools that can be used to analyze student data and use that information to help students achieve success.

# FOURTEEN

## Instructional Interventions

Formative assessment provides a means by which students can "press the reset button," allowing teachers to know where students are in the learning process and informing their instruction. Formative assessment allows you to take the opportunity to stop, if necessary, reflect, and reteach. For many teachers, reteaching means repeating the same information, only louder. In this chapter we will discuss a number of instructional interventions that can be implemented to design instruction or reteach concepts, including flexible grouping, tiered lessons, activities for building automaticity, leveled instructional materials, and scaffolding instruction.

### OVERVIEW: APPLYING WHAT YOU'VE LEARNED

After evaluating student performance and determining what students know and what they still need to learn, we need to then decide what should be retaught. Based on individual student performance, we will need to determine what to do next for the student and what feedback will best meet their needs. Based on group performance (high, middle, and low), we will need to consider our next instructional step.

First, good instruction starts with good curriculum. The curriculum we teach needs to be valid, relevant, and appropriate for the students in the class. Many times we think that just because it is in the textbook the information we are sharing with our students is valid, relevant, and appropriate. If you've been teaching long enough, you've found that this is not always the case. Information presented can be incorrect. It may be written at a level inappropriate for our students. The needs of our students vary as well. We can't rely on the text to supply the curriculum. We need to use what we know about our students and the standards we need to address to define the curriculum we deliver in class.

We need to continually assess our students and compress the curriculum when appropriate. Additionally, we should not feel that we have to teach everything to every student. Some students in our class will already have certain skills. We need to help them move forward rather than holding them back with the rest of the students.

Other students may not have the ability to master every standard. We need to adjust the curriculum and our instruction based on the needs of high- to low-performing students. To do this, we need to identify key skills that all students should have to be able to move on. We need to be prepared to provide additional support for students who still haven't developed those skills and provide paths for advanced students so that all students will be able to move forward.

A community of support should be developed in our classroom. We need to help the students realize that while we are all different, we can all be good at different activities. While one student may not be great in math, he or she may have skill in reading or music or some other activity. We are not all the same, but we all have value—and our students need to respect that value in each other. Students can learn from one another.

A colleague once paired a gifted education student with a learning disabled student for a team project to be completed in a computer science class. The students were creating geometric patterns on the computer. While the gifted student understood the mathematics, he did not understand the visual spatial relationship to create the patterns and three-dimensional objects. The learning disabled student understood and was able to apply these visual spatial concepts intuitively. It was a learning opportunity for both of them.

## FOCUSING ON FOUNDATIONAL KNOWLEDGE

To promote student success, students must be well grounded in the foundational knowledge and skills of the discipline they are studying. Without those foundational skills, students will not be able to progress far in their understanding of more complex constructs. If they are missing a key skill, their growth will be limited, especially when the key skill is foundational to all learning.

The most important skills for students to learn are those that foster learning in all content areas: the abilities to read, write, and compute. These skills are at the base of every content area. We use reading and writing in all instructional fields. Basic computational skills are the foundation of mathematics and science, and they are implemented in other content fields as students learn how to problem solve and how to think.

As we look at how we design instruction and the instructional strategies we implement, we need to focus on these universal foundational skills as well as those constructs that provide the foundation in the discipline being taught. As we identify these basic skills, we need to address students' individual learning needs as they relate to those skills.

We can differentiate instruction so that we can accommodate those learning needs. If students are reading below grade level, we can provide instructional materials that will meet their needs, without holding them back from learning the content. If students take so much time processing information or doing basic arithmetic that they lose track of the meaning, then we need to provide them with cues and supports that will allow them to not get stuck on the basics and learn the larger concept. We also need to take time to help them learn those skills and become fluent with the content, so that the lack of certain foundational skills is no longer a stumbling block.

## THE ROLE OF DIFFERENTIATED INSTRUCTION

So, how can instruction be individualized when one teacher is teaching thirty students or more? It is not unusual for special education teachers to develop individualized lessons for each of their students. Some special education teachers working with learning disabled students design twenty or more individual lesson plans on a daily basis. For most teachers, this would not be manageable—especially for secondary teachers who work with as many as 140 or more students in a day.

Differentiated instruction provides teachers with the means to address these individual needs in a manageable way. Differentiated instruction is designed to provide multiple paths to address the overarching goal of a lesson. By differentiating instruction, you can address the learning needs of all students and achievement can be enhanced (Koeze 2007; Stavroula 2011). Instruction can be differentiated based on the content being taught, the processes implemented during instruction, and the products developed by students to demonstrate their learning.

When using data from formative assessments to differentiate instruction, we will be differentiating based on the readiness of the student for the instruction. By identifying the foundational skills the student is missing, we can adapt the content, process, or product to accommodate these prerequisite skills, providing additional support to help students build these skills, or using our knowledge of the students' skill level to take them to a higher level.

*Content*

To differentiate a lesson based on readiness, the content could be differentiated according to the student's background knowledge and the skills he or she brings to the classroom. The content could be delivered at a level that best meets the readiness level of the student, providing varied readings based on the student's reading ability or the depth of his or her prior knowledge about the content being taught.

In teaching a unit on the Civil War, we could provide materials and resources for learning activities presented at the varying reading/readiness levels of our students. Materials on the Civil War are available from early elementary levels through graduate school. If students are reading at the fourth-grade level in a high school class, reading materials at that level could be obtained. Likewise, if students are reading at the college level, readings will likely also be available at that higher level, which will challenge the students and their thinking.

*Process*

The process used for instructional activities can also be varied based on the learning needs of students. We can look at student readiness, as well as other factors that influence how students learn best. Most students are capable of learning using almost any mode of learning or learning style, but students will learn more readily if the process that is utilized aligns closely with their learning style (Cassidy 2004; Dunn et al. 1990; Dunn, Beaudry, and Klavas 1989; Wang 2006).

One means of differentiating process is designing learning activities that would allow students to learn content while using varying processes that align with their preferred learning style. In designing a unit on cellular biology, you might create parallel learning activities that are based on varied learning styles.

You could vary the process by developing learning opportunities in which students can utilize manipulatives to discover a concept, receive direct instruction from the teacher, or work in pairs to research the concept. A video lecture on the impact of water pollution on the development of a single-cell organism could be presented. Or reading materials on the topic could be provided. Or students could complete a hands-on experiment in which they gather local water samples, making observations on environmental conditions and life within the water samples collected.

Using formative and preassessment data, teachers can compact instruction for students, requiring them to complete learning activities focused specifically on the skills or content they have not yet mastered. Students who have demonstrated mastery for all competencies would move on to the next unit, or instruction from the current unit would be presented at a higher level, engaging the students with more complex concepts.

One might choose to design the course around individualized or small group modules, allowing students to only complete instructional activities related to the competencies they have not yet mastered. After completing the learning activities, students could demonstrate mastery by completing a posttest or other assessment activity. Implementing instruction in this manner would likely involve a whole course redesign, but it can be an effective approach for dealing with classes that include students with a broad range of skills and abilities.

## Product

Allowing the student to select the product to be submitted to demonstrate learning is one means of differentiating instruction. The product could range from writing a persuasive essay or a play to creating a video game. A student could demonstrate his or her knowledge of mammals by writing the traditional research paper, developing a poster presentation, creating a flash video game, or creating a guided instructional activity like a Web quest. At times the teacher will need to differentiate the product based on readiness—identifying a particular level at which they want the student to be working.

Using a tic-tac-toe system works well to support this type of differentiated learning activity. In designing a tic-tac-toe activity, a 9 x 9 matrix is created. Each column could include activities that address different learning outcomes related to the same topic, learning styles, or level of readiness. For example, in designing a tic-tac-toe activity for a geography class, students might be able to choose from creating a brochure advertising the country they are researching, developing a presentation, developing a game, or drawing a map. A tic-tac-toe matrix for a U.S. history class might look like the example in table 14.1.

**Table 14.1.   Tic Tac Toe Example**

| Writing | Technology/Creative | Artisitic/Creative |
|---|---|---|
| Create and deliver a presentation to the class about the country you have selected. | Create a brochure advertising the country you have selected. | Draw a map of the country you have selected labeling key cities and industry in the country. |
| Write a children's story book placed in the country you have selected. Make sure the book is culturally accurate and age appropriate. | Develop a game which engages players in a situation set in the country you have selected. The game should be based on a historically accurate event and a problem the players must address. | Develop a poster which reviews a historical event which took place in the country you have selected. Include images, statistics, and quotes from relevant participants in the event. |

| | | |
|---|---|---|
| Identify a current political or economic issue the country you have selected is facing and write a five paragraph essay explaining the issue and at least two different perspectives about the issue. | Create an instructional website which addresses a current political or economic issue the country you have selected is facing. Provide relevant detail and engage users in an interactive search to learn more about the issue. | Identify a current political or economic issue the country you have selected is facing and develop a visual and auditory presentation to be delivered either electronically or face to face to the class. Explain the issue in detail and at least two different perspectives regarding the issue. |

In completing the tic-tac-toe learning activity, students would complete three of the activities: three across, three down, or three on the diagonal. This type of activity allows students to vary the products they will submit to demonstrate their learning, and to choose activities that align with their learning preferences. This type of arrangement will also work with fewer choices. Three options could be presented, from which students can select one. In one assignment students could choose to view a video and complete a reflection log on the video, they could observe an event or situation and track specific data, or they could do a literature review on the topic being studied. What's important is providing opportunities for choice.

Differentiating instruction is very doable, but developing the materials can be time consuming. Once the decision to differentiate instruction has been made, the temptation is to differentiate everything all at the same time. To make the process more workable it needs to be done gradually, a piece at a time. We need to start with one activity or unit and be selective.

We should differentiate those things that will have the greatest impact on student learning. Differentiate resources, so that over time the curriculum is differentiated, thereby allowing us to support learning at those key points where it is most needed. Differentiated instruction is built up through the need for quality curriculum, a community that supports and values diversity in learning abilities, and the use of formative assessment.

## ASSESSING LEARNER CHARACTERISTICS

In our instruction we need to be aware of the learner characteristics that our students bring to the classroom. We can evaluate our students' readiness, learning style, attitudes, and interests prior to developing and delivering instruction. In this section we will look at methods to learn more about the characteristics our students bring to the classroom.

## Readiness Assessments

Assessing a student's readiness to learn new concepts and constructs can be challenging, and a teacher-created assessment may not be sophisticated enough to do the job. Assessing students' readiness can encompass everything from reading level to required prior knowledge. A number of short-cycle assessments are available that assess the students' reading ability, such as Accelerated Reader, Star Reading, Pro-Ohio, e NWEA MAP, Riverside Assess2Learn, Pearson Learnia, Scholastic, Discovery, and ACT Compass.

As outlined in chapter 4, to assess students' prior knowledge you can develop pretests that focus on the basic knowledge and skills necessary to being able to learn and understand the content to be taught. For example, when teaching students to factor quadratic equations, you need to be sure students know prime numbers, how to factor, and the distributive property.

You will find that students will perform better with new content if they already have the foundational skills necessary to be successful. The preassessment allows you to find out if they have those skills and to remind them of those skills before diving into something new. Many times students do have the prior knowledge—but if we don't take the time to trigger that knowledge, they will not think to apply what they already know to something new.

You can assess for learning skills and prior knowledge as a tool to group students according to their level of readiness and design instruction to meet the students' needs at the appropriate level. The data gathered from these assessments should not be your only determiner in grouping students; allow groupings to be flexible, grouping students on occasion by other means, such as interest or learning style.

## Learning Style Inventories

Assessing students' learning styles goes in and out of fashion. It's true that students are capable of learning without using their preferred learning style, but by the same token, students are more likely to be engaged if you do allow them to use their preferred learning style at least at some point during the lesson. Assessing learning styles at the beginning of the semester will allow you to utilize this information in the design of instruction throughout the school year. While this information does not necessarily provide direct information regarding content knowledge, these assessments will provide you with the tools necessary to support student engagement and promote active student learning by addressing their learning preferences.

There are quick and easy assessments for multiple intelligences and personality types. A variety of measures are available to assess learning style, ranging from simplistic assessments, such as the multiple intelligence assessment offered on the Edutopia website (www.edutopia.org), which consists of twenty-four questions and takes five minutes to complete, to more complex assessments such as the Myers-Briggs Personality Type Indicator (MBTI), which identifies sixteen different personality types. At its basic level, learning styles have been identified to include auditory, visual, and kinesthetic. These can also be easily differentiated into social and independent learners. A variety of quick and easy assessments are available online, for free and for purchase.

Visual learners prefer using images, drawings, maps, and advance organizers to organize information. To support these learners, implement visuals to support your instruction; make use of concept maps, diagrams, pictures, and other visuals to demonstrate concepts or skills being taught. Encourage students to picture words or concepts in their heads, or create drawings that help them better visualize a concept.

Students who prefer a verbal style generally find it easy to express themselves both in writing and verbally. We need to encourage these students to talk themselves through processes, using verbal cues to recall the next step in a procedure or to clarify information for themselves. Make use of mnemonics and music to help them memorize information. Be specific in your instruction. These students generally perform well with direct instruction and lecture. Encourage them to take notes and to read the information back to themselves as they study.

Kinesthetic or physical learners learn by using their hands and bodies, incorporating movement and hands-on learning during instruction. These students need to be moving; they may appear to not be paying attention, but in reality they are hearing every word. They like to work things out with their hands, rather than reading or looking at diagrams to figure something out. The use of manipulatives, hands-on experiments, role-plays, building dioramas, and so on is important to the learning of these students. Even in content areas where the use of tools such as these is not supported, by allowing these students to move and be active during instruction we will support their learning.

Learning styles can be another source for grouping students. Ideally, we need to take the time to design instruction to address students' preferred learning styles. Yes, students can learn in the non-preferred modes, but learning is enhanced when students are engaged using their preferred learning style.

## Attitude and Interest Surveys

Attitude and interest surveys can be utilized at the beginning of a semester to learn more about what is important to your students and their interests as they relate to a unit of study, thereby giving you an anchor to which you can tie instruction. You might begin a unit on poetry with a survey such as the one shown in figure 14.1.

If you can make the content you are teaching relevant to your students, they are more likely to become active participants in the teaching/learning process. With the instrument pictured in figure 14.2, you could utilize examples of poetry that portray activities the students are interested in. We could encourage students to write about the activities they enjoy or utilize symbolism they can relate to. Interest and attitude surveys serve as a tool to increase students' motivation to learn, so that we can engage them in topics that they may not inherently find interesting.

You can also gather information about students' interests by watching them as they interact with other students or with younger children, while they are out on the playground. By listening to their conversations and interacting with them, building a relationship, and learning about what they are interested in outside of school, you can use your knowledge to integrate those interests into what you are teaching. Just as with other preassessments, identifying students' interests and attitudes as related to various aspects of the content can be used as a tool to engage students in instruction.

## INTERVENTIONS

To meet the needs of our students we need to employ multiple instructional strategies. Variety is the key. You can bore anyone with anything—even computers—if you try hard enough. There is no one teaching meth-

I like:

- Hiking in the woods     ☐ Never ☐ Sometimes ☐ Every Chance I Get

- Playing outside     ☐ Never ☐ Sometimes ☐ Every Chance I Get

- Reading stories     ☐ Never ☐ Sometimes ☐ Every Chance I Get

- Listening to music     ☐ Never ☐ Sometimes ☐ Every Chance I Get

- Singing     ☐ Never ☐ Sometimes ☐ Every Chance I Get

- Driving in a car     ☐ Never ☐ Sometimes ☐ Every Chance I Get

- Riding a motorcycle     ☐ Never ☐ Sometimes ☐ Every Chance I Get

- Riding my bike     ☐ Never ☐ Sometimes ☐ Every Chance I Get

**Figure 14.1.    Attitude Interest Survey for a Unit on Poetry**

od that will work for every student. Hence, we need to incorporate variety. Each student should be allowed to experience their preferred learning style every once in a while.

We need to work to design lessons that approximate their readiness level. Students should be allowed to expand on their interests in our classroom. You can have students learn to write a five-paragraph essay in a boring way, or you can make it interesting by allowing students to write about a topic that they find interesting. We need to spice up our classroom and still be able to address the standards we must address. The following sections provide an overview of instructional interventions that can be implemented to support learning by all students.

## Flexible Grouping

Tracking of students has been a practice long implemented in an attempt to support student learning by creating homogenous groups, the idea being that if students are grouped according to ability, instruction can be targeted at the appropriate level. In theory, there is a strong argument for ability grouping. If instruction is provided based upon the learners' readiness level, student learning should be enhanced. Unfortunately, such tracked programs often become a dumping ground in which students are left to flounder with poor instruction, low expectations, a negative stigma, and nothing to motivate them to work toward achieving at higher levels.

Instead of tracking students, a flexible grouping system employed within a heterogeneous classroom provides students with an opportunity to learn from one another and to take advantage of high-quality instruction for all students. Flexible grouping creates temporary groups for a class hour, a week, or a month. It does not create permanent groups.

Rather than grouping students only on ability, flexible grouping allows groups to shift. Sometimes groups shift based on ability and other times because of interest or learning style—or they can just be selected randomly. Student groups should shift based upon the activity and the learning goal. Sometimes you may want the groups to be heterogeneous; at other times you may want them to be homogeneous.

Groups may be designed for a specific activity, and members may be selected based upon specialized skills. Sometimes you may want students to be able to share skills at which they excel with their classmates. If you allow groupings in classroom to flow, changing as needed, students will be able to excel in different areas and will not be trapped in a limiting system. Groups should be organized, shifted, and dissolved as teaching and learning needs change, allowing for maximum flexibility, avoiding the static nature of tracking (Ford 2005).

Groups can be determined based upon a number of factors. Students may be assigned to groups based upon the level of support they need with the content. If students are reading a chapter from the textbook, some students will be able to read and respond independently, while others will need a written reading guide, and still others will need direct support from the teacher. The teacher will be able to work with this small group of students by addressing their learning needs while the rest of the class works independently. This gives these students the opportunity to develop the foundational reading skills they need while also learning the more complex concepts that come more easily to their classmates, meeting the same expectations.

Students may also be grouped based upon the complexity of the task to be completed. We can vary groups based upon skills and abilities that may or may not be directly related to the content being studied. Groups may also be formed to complete a group learning task. With a learning activity such as the reenactment of an event in history, students may be asked to work as actors, videographers, writers, costumers, and so on. Each role assigned is based on skill or interest rather than content ability, but all students learn about the event and the historical context.

In a science class, a jigsaw reading activity might be assigned based upon the complexity of each of the concepts being studied. You might also consider grouping students based upon their reading level. Books on the same topic but written at different levels can be used to group students. While students are all learning the same information, they are doing so at a reading level that best meets their needs.

*Tiered Lessons*

Tiered lessons provide a wonderful tool for addressing a wide range of needs. A tiered lesson is primarily designed to differentiate based upon readiness, but it can be used to differentiate based upon interest and learning style as well. Teachers use tiered lessons so that all students in the class focus on essential understandings and skills but at different levels of complexity, abstractness, and open-endedness.

In designing a tiered lesson you should identify the standards you will be addressing, the key concept you will be teaching, and general ideas and principles, and develop one or more essential questions. The essential questions or understandings are the overarching, big ideas that encompass the learning objectives you are trying to teach. It is the why of why we are learning these skills and concepts.

Next, you will tier the lesson. With a little thought, almost any classroom activity can be tiered: assignments, activities, centers and stations, learning contracts, assessments, materials, experiments, writing prompts, or homework. Two or three tiers is usually best for implementation. However, a teacher who is experienced and comfortable with the strategy may have more tiers if it facilitates the instruction or better meets the needs of the students.

After identifying the key concepts and understandings that you want students to learn, you need to determine the readiness levels of the students and design tasks that will help them master the key concepts while still challenging the students at their level of understanding. We also need to identify what we want our students to be able to do with the information and skills they have learned. Attaching specific skills provides additional meaning to the instruction, helping students understand how what they have learned is utilized by others in their jobs and in everyday life.

We need to create the big picture that brings together all the individual pieces we are teaching. For example, a unit on the Oregon Trail could address the five w's of journalism, writing a five-paragraph essay, journaling, geography, and the mathematical formula for rate x time = distance. But the overarching big idea, or the essential question, you may want to address could be, "How was the western frontier populated and what has been the continuing impact on society today?" These activities could then be tiered according to three different readiness levels. Materials, resources, and individual activities would be designed to meet the various learning needs of the students working at each level.

First, design the basic lesson to be delivered to all students. Here you would design the learning activities to be used with the middle of the road in mind. The challenge is to develop "respectful" activities that are interesting, engaging, and challenging. No student should look at the task and say to himself or herself, "I guess I'm in the dumb group." Then design the other tracks, providing additional support for lower-level students and taking the content to a higher level for those students who need a greater level of challenge.

We need to clone the activity so as to ensure that students are challenged at an appropriate level and realistic success can be achieved. We need to be sure to explain the details to these students, provide examples, and design learning activities at the appropriate level to reinforce the learning. Materials should be designed for basic to advanced levels of performance. We also need to transition content from familiar to unfamiliar. Some tasks in each tier may be the same, while others might be changed to match student readiness levels.

The key to developing good tiered activities is designing them so that they are just above the level of the learner. This helps students stretch and build from where they are. Challenging and supporting students at their level of understanding will help them become successful learners.

## Building Automaticity

Long-term academic success is closely tied to the student's fluency with basic skills such as math facts and reading. Being able to read or perform basic arithmetic quickly and fluently leads to higher levels of comprehension. When students don't need to pause and think about how the next word is pronounced, or contemplate the next step in a process, they are able to focus more completely on the meaning of the text or the process they are performing. Automaticity builds strength in learning, helping students grasp meanings and learn higher-level concepts.

Fluency is built with repeated exposure to the basic skills, which requires the students to demonstrate the skill quickly. We can build student skill by involving them in games in which they work to increase the speed with which they can complete the task, such as word recognition. This can be done by using a short period of time out of each instructional day to engage students with an activity or game that requires them to work with a specific skill that can foster fluency and automaticity. Students can race to complete timed drills of basic math facts, identify parts of speech, or complete a simple process. Flashcards can also be a useful tool. We should begin with flashcards that provide support for concepts in which the student is beginning to develop competence. As the student becomes confident and fluent, we can transition to cards dealing with related concepts of gradually increasing difficulty.

More complex skills such as reading will require more extended exposure, providing students with opportunities to read material that is within their zone of proximal development. We can teach students the cues that can help them process information more quickly. As we teach we can make use of practices such as reading aloud, pronunciation models, and the use of audio materials to support reading abilities. Similar strategies can be used in science, history, and math as we work to increase students' ability to master the core skills that will help them master learning skills as well as content knowledge.

### Leveled Instructional Materials

Leveled materials are instructional materials that are written at multiple reading levels but address the same instructional objectives. In content areas in which students are required to read and comprehend a fair amount of material, it's important that you as the teacher know the reading level of your text and the students' reading ability. If the text is far above or far below the students' reading level, it can cause you as the teacher huge problems, especially in the area of classroom management and engaging the students in what you are trying to teach.

As the teacher you can support students in their reading by obtaining readings written at the appropriate level. Some textbook companies are now providing texts written at multiple levels, and organizations like National Geographic, Teacher-Created Materials, Newbridge Publishing, and NASA have provided instructional materials on their websites written at various levels. Shell Educational Publishing produces a social studies text that is written at reading levels ranging from first through seventh grade. Pearson publishes a selection of leveled readers for use in the elementary curriculum. Follett also provides specific guided reading resources designed to directly support differentiation through leveled reading materials.

It may be as simple as obtaining textbooks from different grade levels. Because we address similar content at multiple levels, we can access textbooks and other materials for many topics at a range of reading levels. For example, we teach students about the Civil War at the elementary, middle school, high school, and college level. It would be fairly easy to obtain reading material for students that more closely aligns with their reading level. If you have a middle school student who is already reading and understanding at the college level, you can provide that student with a textbook or articles that more closely align with their academic ability.

Likewise, if you've got a student who is still reading at a fourth-grade level and he or she is in a high school class, you can obtain reading materials written at the appropriate level to help him or her grow and close the learning gap. If varied reading materials are not available, develop instructional supports that students can use while reading the text. If texts of varying levels aren't available, you may need to develop vocabulary lists, advance organizers, job aids, or note outlines for the material to be read.

The purpose in providing leveled learning materials is to support struggling learners with materials that address their learning needs. Materials can be written at varied reading levels, like those described above, or they may be available in multiple languages to meet the needs of second language learners. Some textbook series provide audio resources or online support that gives directions orally in English or other languages. The idea is to provide materials for grade-level and advanced readers, as well as simplified language and writing tasks for students who need additional support.

## Scaffolding Instruction

Scaffolding instruction involves breaking up the content and processes to be learned into chunks and then providing a structure to help students master each instructional chunk. The purpose that underlies scaffolding is the need to provide students with support while implementing instruction. Frequently, teachers rely on a demonstration or verbal instruction to teach students a process.

Scaffolding transitions verbal instruction into a support system that walks the student through the process, gradually removing supports until the student can complete the process independently. As students demonstrate increased understanding, they are provided increasingly difficult problems to address using the process. Initially, immediate and specific feedback is provided with the completion of each chunk. As students develop, feedback becomes less frequent and direct, allowing students to develop confidence in their own ability.

When scaffolding instruction, we begin first by modeling or describing the concept or skill at least three times, verbalizing our own thought processes as we implement the process. During instruction we show students what we expect the outcome of their work to look like. Ideally an example is presented to students, along with the rubric or criteria that will be used to evaluate the product.

We should make use of graphic organizers, pictures, or tools to help guide the students through the process we are teaching. We can use these to help guide the students through the process step by step. In essence, these resources can serve as a job aid, cuing students to the next step in the process.

As students work toward learning the process, we need to monitor their progress, checking for understanding at each step, questioning students, and helping them develop an understanding as to why they are completing each step. It's important that students understand the purpose of each step and why each is completed, instead of becoming overreliant on the scaffolding. It is essential that learners use these tools to build confidence in their own ability.

Scaffolding provides an effective way for students to develop skill and confidence in completing complex tasks. As you work with students while scaffolding instruction, you can reinforce learning, revise instruction, provide corrective feedback, and emphasize specific elements that may be a cause for confusion for the learner. When you provide detailed instructional support and scaffold student learning, the students' confidence with the content gradually builds, and you help students become independent learners.

## HOLD LEARNING CONSTANT AND LET TIME VARY

If integrated early enough in the learning process, instructional strategies such as those described within this chapter can increase learning significantly, making these strategies worth the time it takes to implement them in the instructional process. They can increase learning, allowing us to more efficiently and effectively work to hold learning constant and let time vary. When we work to implement strategies that are implemented in the classroom based on formative assessment data, students can quickly master information and ideas. We can also hold learning constant and let time vary for students who need more time to reach the desired level of mastery.

As we implement instruction based on formative assessment, we need to make sure that we match the task to the student. We need to take into consideration a student's individual skills and abilities in addition to those required by the learning activity. It is okay for students to complete different work. Fair is not equal—it is every student getting what he or she needs. We often need to be more a coach than a teacher.

Just as a football, tennis, basketball, or softball coach will work with the team helping them develop the skills that they need to win, you need to coach your students to academic success. Students need to know that you have faith and confidence in their ability to learn. You need to believe in them. When learning becomes a collaboration between teacher and students, you will be able to truly coach your students to the point where learning becomes the focus. Time is allowed to vary and learning is held constant.

## CONCLUSION

In this chapter we have discussed a variety of instructional strategies that can be implemented to address learning issues that have been identified through formative assessment. As we utilize formative assessment to inform instruction, we need to not just reteach the same lesson, but we need to look at the concepts differently. We need to get our students to look at the concepts differently.

By focusing on the foundational skills that are necessary for students to learn, including reading, writing, and arithmetic, we can help students become successful learners and get beyond those skills that so frequently act as stumbling blocks for learning. To address our students' learning needs and to bring a new perspective to the content that we are teaching, we need to differentiate instruction. We can differentiate instruction based upon readiness, interest, and learning style by varying the content we teach, the processes we use to teach it, or the product we require students to complete to demonstrate their learning.

In this chapter we reviewed five interventions to address student learning needs: flexible grouping, tiered lessons, activities for building automaticity, leveled instructional materials, and scaffolding instruction. By addressing students' individual learning needs early, based on continuous formative assessment data, we can promote student learning. We can help each student hold learning constant.

# FIFTEEN
## Bringing It All Together

In the end, it's important to help students understand that learning is a matter of trial and error. We learn best from our mistakes. "If I fail that's okay—I can press the reset button and start over." We, on the other hand, need to learn the importance of multiple assessments. The need to utilize multiple assessments in evaluating student learning in terms of summative assessment permeates the literature (Brookhart 2009). We seldom take into consideration the need to implement multiple assessments, using a variety of formats and methods, as we guide the learning process.

In this chapter we will bring the idea of using formative assessment as a tool to inform instruction and press the reset button full circle. We will discuss teaching students how to learn from their failures and how to make use of multiple assessments to inform instruction throughout the teaching and learning process.

### LEARNING HOW TO LEARN

The formative assessment process is a collaboration between teachers and students. To make this an effective collaboration, attention must be paid to teaching students how to use information gathered from formative assessments, as well as teacher and peer feedback, to support their own learning—along with using formative assessment to inform the instructional practices we implement. We need to teach all students how to learn. We need to teach them how to learn from failure.

We are not just teaching students content in our classrooms. We also try to teach them to take personal responsibility for their own successes and failures. We teach students how to communicate, work as a team, and implement critical thinking and problem-solving skills. We also should teach students social skills such as respecting differences and sup-

153

porting change, and about the rewards of becoming lifelong learners (Gardiner 1994). One of the greatest skills we can give our students is the ability to learn independently and be intentional learners (Wirth and Perkins 2008).

Ideally, we will be able to teach students to diagnose their own learning needs and then make specific learning goals for themselves, identify resources to support their learning, select and implement learning strategies, and evaluate their own learning. Developing these skills is actually a lifelong process, but we can work with our students to make strides toward this level of motivation.

We need to take the time to teach our students about time management, note taking, how to annotate their textbook as they read, and other study skills. These are skills that can benefit every student. However, key to moving students toward becoming intentional learners is realizing that significant learning is characterized by change in their behaviors and motivations (Fink 2003).

We need to design instruction to ensure that significant learning is taking place. Rather than focusing on surface learning, we need to promote deep learning in which students find and use knowledge rather than just memorize information. This happens when students are engaged in active learning.

> A classic study of the National Training Board found that students retained only 5% of the information they received in lecture, twenty-four hours later. Retention rates increased to 75–90% when active learning involving peer teaching was used instead of lectures. Other active learning methods (e.g., demonstration and discussion) also resulted in higher retention rates (30% and 50%, respectively). (Wirth and Perkins 2008)

How we approach teaching will help our students learn how to learn. As we teach, we need to make sure our students have a clear understanding of the scope of what we are working to learn. Not only do we need to inform students of our learning goals for them, but we also need to work with them to develop their own learning goals for the content being taught. We need to know our content and be enthusiastic about our content. Our students will know when we are bored or frustrated. If you find yourself teaching a topic about which you are not enthusiastic, "fake it until you make it."

Our students will be less motivated if they know we don't like what we are teaching. We also need to be clear. If we cannot explain a concept or process simply, we do not know it well enough. Our expectations, our directions, and our teaching must be clear and understood by our students. We need to guide our students to resources that will help them achieve their personal learning goals, as well as the learning outcomes we've identified. These goals and outcomes need to be specific, clear, and developmentally appropriate. We need to work with students so that they know their strengths and weaknesses and are able to write personal goals that will help them achieve success.

We need to provide students with opportunities to interact with the content, with each other, and with us. Collaborative learning is an excellent tool for engaging students in active learning. It promotes academic achievement, the development of metacognition, and a "willingness to assume difficult tasks, persistence, motivation, and transfer of learning to new situations" (Wirth and Perkins 2008).

As we teach we need to be prepared to adjust our teaching on the fly, to deepen student understanding and to address misconceptions. In our preparation we need to plan the questions we will ask during class discussions to focus students on important concepts and to engage the students. We need to use provocative questions that will promote self-reflection by students on their understanding of the content and their own performance. Questions should be planned to help students focus on the criteria they will need to meet in order to be successful.

Feedback that is clear, descriptive, and task specific should be used to help students monitor where they are in relation to the learning goals and outcomes that have been identified. This feedback can further be supported if we take the time to describe student learning along a continuum of progress toward reaching the learning goal. We can plan ahead to adjust instruction and identify ways to support students who need varying levels of support to be successful.

We should be prepared to model self-assessment for our students. As we teach, we need to demonstrate the kinds of reasoning and thinking skills that students will need to implement in order to be successful. During instruction, teach specific metacognitive strategies to maximize student success, such as outlining, concept mapping, self-testing, situational awareness, planning and monitoring, and reflection.

Finally, we can give students the opportunity to put what they are learning into practice. They need to be allowed to try and, yes, sometimes fail. We want them to try to apply what they've learned. If they fail we need to work with them to figure out what they did wrong. Learning through our failures is good only when it teaches us things we couldn't have learned otherwise. When we engage our students in active learning and give them opportunities to try and to fail, our students will learn the content to greater depth and they will learn how they learn best.

The key to teaching our students how to learn is to change the way they think about learning. Rather than seeing themselves as students being taught, they need to see themselves as researchers gathering information on a subject they want to learn about (Sonmez 2012). Trying and failing is how researchers learn (Sonmez 2012). Once our students have researched and figured out how to actually apply what they've learned, we then need to give them lots of time to practice and gain experience. As our students become skilled learners and are able to use metacognitive strategies to support their own learning, they will gain confidence and become more independent, intentional learners.

## ROLE OF MULTIPLE ASSESSMENTS

The purpose of assessment is to elicit and gather evidence of learning. Just as students learn differently and more easily excel with different instructional strategies, students can also excel with different forms of assessment. When we rely on only one form of assessment, we short-change students who do not test as well with that form. By using multiple assessments, we will have a greater understanding of the breadth and depth of our students' learning.

Each learning objective we teach has multiple dimensions. To assess students' learning based on those dimensions, we need to examine their learning from multiple perspectives. Those multiple perspectives are gained by using a variety of methods to observe and collect data on our students' learning, as described in chapters 4 through 12.

The real value of multiple measures becomes evident when you examine the standards and objectives we are supposed to be teaching. Those standards provide the guidelines we need to follow when assessing student learning. There needs to be a clear alignment between the standards and learning goals and the assessments we use to document student learning, and how we teach students these constructs.

If our learning objective requires students to be able to present information, then the assessment we have selected should involve students in presenting information. If our learning objective requires students to be able to identify something, then the assessment can be a simple multiple choice quiz in which the student identifies the correct answer. If our learning objective requires students to be able to synthesize information, then the assessment needs to require that students synthesize information. Alignment needs to be evident.

## MAKING IT WORKABLE

As you implement the formative assessment process in your classroom, you need to remember to keep it workable. If things become too complex and time consuming, you will not be able to maintain the process. Keep things simple, coordinated, and useful. Begin by planning for assessment. You need to review the standards and objectives that you will be teaching and prioritize them. Build formative assessments for those indicators that are critical to student success as they progress in their development and understanding of the discipline.

Formative assessment should become part of your routine, so that students understand your expectations and are able to quickly and efficiently finish the assigned task. Design assessment tasks that are focused on one or perhaps two learning objectives, so they can be assessed and analyzed quickly. It is important to develop a log sheet that you can use to track student data. If possible, take the time to score and record activities that are to be used as formative assessments at the time they are completed in class.

To increase the likelihood that formative assessment will become part of your routine, simplify the tools and rubrics that will be used to score the assessment. Organize your records so that scores are grouped by the learning objectives and indicators they assess. Color code scores, so that at a glance you can see where students are in their performance. Make use of technology to track student performance and record observations and feedback. Format tools so that it is easy to examine individual student data as well as whole group performance.

## "PRESS THE RESET BUTTON" METAPHOR

The gaming experience gives us a clear outline of what our classrooms should be like in order to enhance learning (Linder 2012). They provide a model of strategies we can employ in our classrooms to help students "press the reset button." Video games let players practice without penalty, with an infinite number of chances to move on to the next level. These games also reward the players for their perseverance. Players also get immediate, descriptive feedback during the entire time they play. As they play, their actions have immediate impact. As they turn the wheel of their car or change the angle of trajectory of a missile, they immediately see the consequences of their actions.

As we design learning activities we need to create opportunities for students to have similar experiences. We need to make use of guided practice so students can have immediate descriptive feedback. For example, in a math class we can implement guided practice by demonstrating how to solve a problem for the students. The students would then be given one or two problems to solve as the teacher walks around the room and monitors their progress.

Immediate feedback is given to students as they work, and also after students have finished the problem. The teacher brings the class back together and works through the problem with the students, checking for understanding. Students who understand how to work the problems are let loose to begin working problems independently. Students who are still having difficulties would work though a few more guided practice problems. As they master the skill, they begin working independently, which allows the teacher to work with a smaller group of students who really need direct support. This mirrors to some extent the experiences players have with a video game.

As you learn the tools of the game you learn that each has a different purpose. Each tool has strengths and weaknesses. The different strategies you employ might require different tools. Just as with games, the tools that we use to learn, solve problems, and create new ideas are context specific and are applied differently depending on the situation. As in the game, the purpose and relevance of the tools that are used to actively engage students to create, problem solve, and explore should be evident to the students.

Games have a built-in mechanism to teach players to transfer their knowledge to increasingly difficult problems or different situations. Like students, as players move from level to level as they play the game, they must transfer what they learned previously to the new level. Transfer of knowledge is one of the biggest challenges we face in the classroom.

Transfer occurs when learning in one situation impacts performance in another setting that has different parameters.

> For example, learning to drive a car helps a person at a later time to learn more quickly to drive a truck, learning mathematics prepares students to study physics, learning to get along with one's siblings may prepare one for getting along better with others, and experience playing chess might even make one a better strategic thinker in politics or business. (Perkins and Salomon 1992)

Transfer is enhanced when we provide students with lots of practice with diverse problems and parameters. If we want to improve our students' reading skills, we need to give them time to read and encourage them to read across a variety of genres. As we teach students how to solve problems, we also need to work with them so that they can identify the variables that impact the problem. As they learn how to explicitly identify the issues that impact the problem, they will be better prepared to do the same for different problems.

Students who actively self-monitor their own thinking processes are more able to transfer their learning. We need to not only teach students problem-solving strategies, but also be mindful of the strategies they are applying. Active self-monitoring helps students recognize when they need to apply another strategy. Transfer can also be facilitated when new material is tied to prior knowledge and previous course materials.

By providing a reset button, games do something that we need to do in education. Time is allowed to vary, and learning is held constant and controlled by the players with no time limit. "Impatient learners can forge ahead and try lots of strategies in a short amount of time, while more reflective learners can take as much time as they need to create a plan of action" (Linder 2012). If we use assessments only to assign a grade, they are summative.

If that information is used to improve instruction, reteach, or refine student learning, it becomes a formative assessment. Many tools that we already use in our classrooms, such as collaborative learning, writing activities, and graphic organizers, can also be used to identify areas in which students need to go back and relearn information or skills. "We need to teach students using the concept that gamers have used so well: Failure is okay as long as it leads to learning" (Dirksen 2011). You can let time vary by pressing the reset button in the classroom. It's called formative assessment.

## CONCLUSION

As we build our assessment plan, formatively and summatively, of key importance is aligning the objectives we teach to the assessments we will use to assess student learning. Have you ever taken a test and wondered where the teacher "came up with that?" You're saying to yourself, "When did she teach that?" The problem is alignment. Before a course is taught teachers identify learning objectives, but sometimes they don't teach all of the objectives they have identified—yet they may still try to assess them. So alignment includes not only alignment of the objectives with the assessments, but also alignment with the teaching strategies.

As we align our learning goals and the assessments, we need to make sure that we are using multiple assessment formats. In doing so, we will be able to get a broad picture of our students' capabilities, strengths, and weaknesses. We will be able to stop and take the time to teach our students those things they have not yet mastered, but which are critical to their future success in the discipline. We will be able to learn more about the metacognitive strategies that will best support their efforts to become independent, intentional learners.

# Bibliography

"ACE Strategy." TeacherWeb.com. Accessed January 15, 2013. http://teacherweb.com/NM/BosqueSchool/BLazar/ACEStrategyrev2-09.pdf

Achieve. n.d. "Increasing Achievement for Schools, Teachers, and Students." Accessed January 15, 2013. http://www.achievetest.com/asd/achieve/newhome.htm

Alber, Rebecca. "Six Scaffolding Strategies to Use with Your Students." Edutopia. Last modified March 24, 2011. http://www.edutopia.org/blog/scaffolding-lessons-six-strategies-rebecca-alber

Allrich, Rod. "Zone of Proximal Development." Purdue. Accessed December 19, 2012. http://web.ics.purdue.edu/~rallrich/learn/zone.html

Anderson, Terry. 2003. "Getting the Mix Right Again: An Updated and Theoretical Rationale for Interaction." *International Review of Research in Open and Distance Learning* 4, no. 2.

Angelo, Thomas, and Patricia Cross. 1993. *Classroom Assessment Techniques: A Handbook for College Teachers*. 2nd ed. San Francisco: Jossey-Bass.

Assessment Oversight Policy Development Directorate. 2007. "Testing in the Public Service of Canada: Standards for the Development and Use of Tests for Appointment Purposes." Accessed December 24, 2012. http://www.psc-cfp.gc.ca/plcy-pltq/guides/assessment-evaluation/tips-tapf/tips-tafp-eng.pdf

Ausubel, David P. 1960. "The Use of Advance Organizers in the Learning and Retention of Meaningful Verbal Material." *Journal of Educational Psychology* 51: 267–72.

Ausubel, David P. 1970. "The Use of Ideational Organizers in Science Teaching." Occasional Paper 3. ERIC Document Reproduction Service No. ED 050 930.

Ausubel, David. 1978. "In Defense of Advance Organizers: A Reply to the Critics." *Review of Educational Research* 48: 251–57.

Bernard, Robert M., Philip C. Abrami, Eugene Borokhovski, C. Anne Wade, Rana M. Tamim, Michael A. Surkes, and Edward Clement Bethel. 2009. "A Meta-Analysis of Three Types of Interaction Treatments in Distance Education." *Review of Educational Research* 79, no. 3:1243–1289.

Black, Paul, and Dylan Wiliam. 1998a. "Assessment and Classroom Learning." *Assessment in Education* 51: 7–74.

Black, Paul, and Dylan Wiliam. 1998b. "Inside the Black Box Raising Standards through Classroom Assessment." *Phi Delta Kappan* 80, no. 2: 139–44.

Black, Paul, and Dylan Wiliam. 2006. "The Reliability of Assessments." In *Assessment and Learning*, edited by John Gardner, 119–31. London: Sage.

Bloom, Benjamin S. 1956. "Taxonomy of Educational Objectives, Handbook I: The Cognitive Domain." New York: David McKay.

Brighton, Catherine M. "Preassessment: A Differentiation Power Tool." National Association for Gifted Children. Accessed February 10, 2012. http://www.nagc.org/index2.aspx?id=978

Brookhart, Susan M. 2009. "The Many Meanings of 'Multiple Measures.'" *Educational Leadership* 67, no. 3: 6–12.

Brown, Paul B. 2012. "The One Thing All Successful Entrepreneurs Have in Common . . . and What We All Learn from It." http://www.forbes.com/sites/actiontrumpseverything/2012/06/26/the-one-thing-all-successful-entrepreneurs-have-in-ommon-and-what-everyone-can-learn-from-it/

Brown, Paul B., Charles F. Kiefer, and Leonard A. Schlesinger. 2012. "New Project? Don't Analyze—Act." *Harvard Business Review* 903: 154+.

Brozo, William G., and Michele L. Simpson. 2003. "Readers, Teachers, Learners: Expanding Literacy across the Content Areas." Upper Saddle River, NJ: Merrill Prentice Hall.

Cassidy, Simon. 2004. "Learning Styles: An Overview of Theories, Models, and Measures." *Educational Psychology: An International Journal of Experimental Educational Psychology* 24, no. 4: 419–44.

Clark, Ian F., and Patrick R. James. 2004. "Using Concept Maps to Plan an Introductory Structural Geology Course." *Journal of Geoscience Education* 52: 224–30.

Consensus Research Consortium. 1998. *Consensus Building*. Boulder: University of Colorado. http://www.colorado.edu/conflict/peace/treatment/consens.htm

Cooper, James Michael, ed. 2011. "Classroom Teaching Skills." Belmont, CA: Wadsworth, Cengage Learning.

Cortina, Jose M. 1993. "What Is Coefficient Alpha? An Examination of Theory and Applications." *Journal of Applied Psychology* 781: 98–104.

Covey, Stephen. 1994. *The 7 Habits of Highly Effective People: Powerful Lessons in Personal Change*. London: Simon & Schuster.

Delacruz, Girlie C. 2011. "Games as Formative Assessment Environments: Examining the Impact of Explanations of Scoring and Incentives in Math Learning, Game Performance, and Help Seeking." CRESST Report 796. The National Center for Research on Evaluation, Standards, and Student Testing. Los Angeles: University of California, Los Angeles. http://www.cse.ucla.edu/products/reports/R796.pdf

Devine, Anthony. 2009. "Formative Assessments for English Language Learners." http://marzanoresearch.com/documents/Anthony_Devine.pdf

d'Inverno, Ray, Hugh Davis, and Su White 2003. "Using a Personal Response System for Promoting Student Interaction." *Teaching Mathematics and Its Application* 224: 163–69. http://eprints.soton.ac.uk/259202/1/Using_a_personal_response_system_for_promoting_student_interaction.pdf

Dirksen, Debra J. 2011. "Hit the Reset Button: Use Formative Assessment to Guide Instruction." *Phi Delta Kappan* 927: 26–31.

Dunn, Rita, Jeffrey S. Beaudry, and Angela Klavas. 1989. "Survey of Research on Learning Styles." *Educational Leadership* 46, no. 6: 50–58.

Dunn, Rita, Mary Cecilia Giannitti, John B. Murray, Ino Rossi, Gene Geisert, and Peter Quinn. 1990. "Grouping Students for Instruction: Effects of Learning Style on Achievement and Attitudes." *Journal of Social Psychology* 130, no. 4: 485–94.

Edmentum™ Assessments. 2012. "Measure: Comprehensive Assessment Solutions for Teachers and Students." Bloomington, MN: Edmentum. http://www.edmentum.com/sites/edmentum.com/files/resource/media/0128-31_Assessments.pdf.

Educational Testing Service (ETS). 2003. "Linking Classroom Assessment with Student Learning." http://www.ets.org/Media/Tests/TOEFL_Institutional_Testing_Program/ELLM2002.pdf.

Fink, L. Dee. 2003. "Creating Significant Learning Experiences: An Integrated Approach to Designing College Courses." San Francisco: Jossey-Bass.

Ford, Michael P. 2005. "Differentiation through Flexible Grouping: Successfully Reaching All Readers." Naperville, IL: Learning Point Associates. http://www.learningpt.org/pdfs/literacy/flexibleGrouping.pdf

Foster, David, and Audrey Poppers. 2009. "Using Formative Assessment to Drive Learning—The Silicon Valley Mathematics Initiative: A Twelve-Year Research and Development Project." http://www.svmimac.org/images/Using_Formative_Assessment_to_Drive_Learning_Reduced.pdf.

Foundation/Progressive Policy Institute. 2013. "Datawise." Measured Progress. http://www.measuredprogress.org

Fuchs, Lynn S., and Douglas Fuchs. 1986. "Effects of Systematic Formative Evaluation: A Meta-Analysis." *Exceptional Children* 522: 199–208.

Gardiner, Lion F. 1994. "Redesigning Higher Education: Producing Dramatic Gains in Student Learning." ASHE-ERIC Higher Education Report 7, Washington, DC: George Washington University.

Gardner, Howard. 1993. *Frames of Mind: The Theory of Multiple Intelligences.* New York: Basic Books.

Garies, Christopher R., and Leslie W. Grant. 2008. "Teacher-Made Assessments: How to Connect Curriculum Instruction and Student Learning." Larchmont, NY: Eye on Education.

Herman, Joan L., Ellen Osmundson, Carlos Ayala, Stephen Schneider, and Mike Timms. 2006. "The Nature and Impact of Teachers' Formative Assessment Practices: CSE Technical Report 703." Los Angeles: National Center for Research on Evaluation, Standards, and Student Testing.

Hitton, Shanti. 2013. "How to Write Jeopardy Game Show Questions." eHow. http://www.ehow.com/how_5777335_write-jeopardy-game-show-questions.html

Honey, Margaret. 2007. "The Role of Formative Assessment in Pre-K through Second Grade Classrooms: White Paper." Wireless Generation Inc. http://www.amplify.com/pdf/white-papers/DIB-ELS_Research_FormativeAssessment_WhitePaper_2007_01.pdf

Hopkins, Gary. 2006. "Dictionary Deception." Education World. http://www.educationworld.com/a_lesson/friday/friday024.shtml

Hopkins, Gary. 2009. "Ten Field Day Classroom Games." Education World. http://www.educationworld.com/a_lesson/lesson/field_day_games.shtml

Hopkins, Gary. 2011. "Stage a Debate: A Primer for Teachers Lincoln-Douglas Debate Format." Education World. http://www.educationworld.com/a_lesson/03/lp304-01.shtml

Hudson, J. Nicky, and D. R. Bristow. 2006. "Formative Assessment Can Be Fun as Well as Educational." *Advances in Physiology Education* 30: 33–37.

Imbeau, Marcia B. 2012. "The Importance of Clear Learning Goals and KUDs." Presented at ASCD Conference: "Differentiation Grows Up," Philadelphia, March 21–23, 2012. http://www.caroltomlinson.com/Presentations/2012ASCD_DiffGrowsUp_Imbeau.pdf

Jonsson, Anders, and Gunilla Svingby. 2007. "The Use of Rubrics: Reliability, Validity, and Educational Consequences." *Educational Research Review* 2: 130–44.

Klotz, Mary Beth. 2007. "Response to Intervention RTI: A Primer for Parents." Bethesda, MD: National Association of School Psychologists. http://www.nasponline.org/resources/handouts/revisedPDFs/rtiprimer.pdf

Koeze, Patricia A. 2007. "Differentiated Instruction: The Effect on Student Achievement in an Elementary School." Masters theses and doctoral dissertations, Paper 31. Eastern Michigan University. http://commons.emich.edu/theses/31 2007

Lewis, Eileen, and Elaine Seymour. "Classroom Assessment Techniques: Attitude Surveys." *Field-Tested Learning Assessment Guide for Science, Math, Engineering, and Technology Instructors.* Madison: University of Wisconsin–Madison. Accessed January 15, 2013. http://www.flaguide.org/cat/attitude/attitude7.php

Lexia. "Lexia: The Future of Reading Education." Accessed January 15, 2013. http://www.lexialearning.com/

Linder, Katie. 2012. "What Can Angry Birds Teach Us about Universal Design for Instruction." *The Profhacker: Tips about Teaching, Technology, and Productivity* blog. August 24, 2012. https://chronicle.com/blogs/profhacker/what-can-angry-birds-teach-us-about-universal-design-for-instruction/42038

Looney, Janet. 2010. "Making It Happen: Formative Assessment and Educational Technologies." *Thinking Deeper.* Research Paper No. 1 – Part 3. Promethean Education Strategy Group. http://www.innovationunit.org/sites/default/files/Promethean%20-%20Thinking%20Deeper%20Research%20Paper%20part%203.pdf

Lyon, G. Reid, Jack M. Fletcher, Bennett Shaywitz, Sally Shaywitz, Joseph Torgesen, Frank Wood, Ann Schulte, and Richard Olson. 2001. "Rethinking Learning Disabilities." In *Rethinking Special Education for A New Century*, 259–80. Washington, DC: Thomas B. Fordham.

Maryland State Department of Education (MSDE). 2012. "School Improvement in Maryland: Monitoring Student Progress." http://mdk12.org/data/progress/index.html

Marzano, Robert. 2007. "The Art and Science of Teaching: A Comprehensive Framework for Effective Instruction." Alexandria, VA: Association for Supervision and Curriculum Development.

Mayer, Richard. 2003. *Learning and Instruction*. Upper Saddle River, NJ: Pearson Education.

McCurdy, Barry L., and Edward S. Shapiro. 1992. "A Comparison of Teacher Monitoring, Peer Monitoring, and Self-Monitoring with Curriculum-Based Measurement in Reading among Student with Learning Disabilities." *Journal of Special Education* 262, no. 9: 162–80.

Meyer, Emily, and Louise Z. Smith. 1987. *The Practical Tutor*. New York: Oxford University Press.

MindTools.com. 2012. "Overcoming Fear of Failure: Facing Fears and Moving Forward." Accessed December 18, 2012, http://www.mindtools.com/pages/article/fear-of-failure.htm

More4kinds.info. "Helping Kids Overcome Fear of Failure." Accessed December 19, 2012, http://www.more4kids.info/725/helping-kids-overcome-failure

Morgan, Mel. "Data Tools to Drive Instruction" (paper presented at the meeting of the New Mexico North Central Association Commission on Accreditation and School Improvement Fall conference, Albuquerque, NM., September 19, 2008.

Moss, Connie M., and Susan M. Brookhart. 2009. "Advancing Formative Assessment in Every Classroom: A Guide for Instructional Leaders." Alexandria, VA: ASCD.

Myers-Briggs Foundation. "MBTI Personality Type." Accessed December 12, 2012, http://www.myersbriggs.org/

National Center for Education Evaluation and Regional Assistance (NCEERA). 2009. "Using Student Achievement Data to Support Instructional Decision Making." U.S. Department of Education. http://ies.ed.gov/ncee/wwc/pdf/practice_guides/dddm_pg_092909.pdf

National Center on Student Progress Monitoring. "Common Questions for Progress Monitoring." Accessed December 22, 2012, http://www.studentprogress.org/progresmon.asp#2

National Dissemination Center for Children with Disabilities (NICHCY). 2012. "Response to Intervention (RTI)." Accessed December 21, 2012. http://nichcy.org/schools-administrators/rti#elements

New Mexico Publication Department. 2009. "The Student Assistance Team SAT and the Three-Tier Model of Student Intervention: A Guidance and Resource Manual for New Mexico's Response to Intervention RTI framework." Santa Fe: New Mexico Public Education Department. http://ped.state.nm.us/sat3tier/sat3tierModelComplete.pdf.

Nhouyvanisvong, Adisack. 2011. "Reliability Concerns for Classroom Formative Assessment." *The Naiku Blog*. December 24, 2012. http://www.naiku.net/blog/reliability-concerns-for-classroom-formative-assessment/

Nichols, Beverly W., and Kevin P. Singer. 2000. "Developing Data Mentors." *Educational Leadership* 575: 34–37.

Nicol, David. 2008. "Technology-Supported Assessment: A Review of Research." Unpublished manuscript. http://www.reap.ac.uk/resources.html

Nitko, Anthony J., and Susan M. Brookhart. 2011. *Educational Assessment of Students*. 6th ed. Boston: Pearson.

North Central Regional Educational Laboratory (NCREL). "Reach Consensus." Accessed December 15, 2012. http://www.ncrel.org/sdrs/areas/issues/educatrs/profdevl/pd2reach.htm

Northwest Evaluation Association (NWEA). 2013. "Computer-Based Adaptive Assessments." http://www.nwea.org/

Orchard Now. 2012. "Orchard Now." http://www.orchardnow.com/index.php

Pearson, 2013. "Developmental Reading Assessment, 2nd Education Plus." Accessed http://www.pearsonschool.com.

Peha, Steven. 2003. "Writing across the Curriculum." Teaching That Makes Sense, Inc. http://www.ttms.org/PDFs/06%20Writing%20Across%20the%20Curriculum%20v001%20Full.pdf

Perkins, David N., and Gavriel Salomon. 1992. "Transfer of Learning." In *International Encyclopedia of Education*. 2nd ed. Oxford: Pergamon Press. http://learnweb.harvard.edu/alps/thinking/docs/traencyn.htm

Peterson, Shelley S. 2007. "Teaching Content with the Help of Writing across the Curriculum." *National Middle School Association* 392: 26–33.

Pohl, M. (2000). *Learning to Think, Thinking to Learn: Models and Strategies to Develop a Classroom Culture of Thinking*. Cheltenham, Vic.: Hawker Brownlow.

Popham, James. 2009. "A Process—Not a Test." *Educational Leadership* 667: 85–86.

Preston, Chris, and Lee Mowbray. 2008. "Use of SMART Boards for Teaching, Learning, and Assessment in Kindergarten Science." *Teaching Science— Journal of the Australian Science Teachers Association* 542: 50–53. http://smartboardita.pbworks.com/f/smartboard+with+kindergartener.pdf

readwritethink. 2013. "Double-Entry Journal." International Reading Association and National Council of Teacher of English. http://www.readwritethink.org/classroom-resources/printouts/double-entry-journal-30660.html

Renaissance Learning. 2013. "Star Enterprise." http://www.renlearn.com/se/default.aspx

Ross, John A. 2006. "The Reliability, Validity, and Utility of Self-Assessment." *Practical Assessment, Research and Evaluation* 11, no. 10. http://pareonline.net/pdf/v11n10.pdf

Ruiz-Primo, Maria Araceli, and Erin Marie Furtak. 2006. "Informal Formative Assessment and Scientific Inquiry: Exploring Teachers' Practices and Student Learning." *Educational Assessment* 112: 205–35.

Sadker, David, Myra Sadker, and Karen R. Zittleman. 2011. "Questioning Skills." In *Classroom Teaching Skills*, edited by James Michael Cooper, 109–50. Belmont, CA: Wadsworth, Cengage Learning.

Scantron. 2012. "Performance Series: Web-Based Diagnostics." http://www.scantron.com/performanceseries/.

Scholastic. "Assess DRA Reading Levels." Accessed February 19, 2013, http://www.scholastic.com/parents/resources/article/book-selection-tips/assess-dra-reading-levels

Scriven, Michael. 1991. *Evaluation Thesaurus*, 4th ed. Newbury Park, CA: Sage.

Simon, Cathy Allen. 2013. "Using the Think-Pair-Share Technique." National Council of Teachers of English. http://www.readwritethink.org/professional-development/strategy-guides/using-think-pair-share-30626.html

Simpson, Elizabeth J. 1972. *The Classification of Educational Objectives in the Psychomotor Domain*. Washington, DC: Gryphon House.

Sims, Peter. 2012. "The No. 1 Enemy of Creativity: Fear of Failure." *Harvard Business Review* Blog Network, December 19, 2012, http://blogs.hbr.org/cs/2012/10/the_no_1_enemy_of_creativity_f.html

Smith, Mike U., and Sherry A. Southerland. "Classroom Assessment Techniques: Interviews." *Field-Tested Learning Assessment Guide: For Science, Math, Engineering, and Technology Instructors*. Madison, WI: University of Wisconsin–Madison. http://www.flaguide.org/cat/interviews/interviews7.php

Sonmez, John. 2012. "Making the Complex Simple: Learning to Learn." The *Making the Complex Simple* Blog, September 23, 2012. http://simpleprogrammer.com/2012/09/23/learning-to-learn/

Stavroula, Valiande A., Leonidas, Kyriakides and Mary, Koutselini 2011."Investigating the Impact of Differentiated Instruction in Mixed Ability Classrooms: It's impact on the quality and equity Dimensions of Education Effectiveness." Accessed http://www.icsei.net/icsei2011/Full%20Papers/0155.pdf.

Stiggins, Rick. 2007. "Assessment for Learning: An Essential Foundation of Productive Instruction." In *Ahead of the Curve: The Power of Assessment to Transform Teaching and Learning*, edited by D. Reeves, 59–76. Bloomington, IN: Solution Tree.

Stobart, Gordon. 2011. "Validity in Formative Assessment." In *Assessment and Learning*, edited by John Gardner, 133–46. London: Sage.

Stone, Carol L. 1983. "A Meta-Analysis of Advanced Organizer Studies." *Journal of Experimental Education* 517: 194–99.

Swan, Karen, Jia Shen, and Starr R. Hiltz. 2006. "Assessment and Collaboration in Online Learning." *Journal of Asynchronous Learning Networks* 101: 45–62. http://www-new.kent.edu/ehhs/dl/upload/assessment-and-collaboration.pdf

Szeto, Joanna. 2010. "Improve Vocabulary and Comprehension by Playing Password." Examiner.com. http://www.examiner.com/article/improve-vocabulary-and-comprehension-by-playing-password

Texas Education Agency and University of Texas System. 2010. "TPRI Early Reading Assessment." http://www.tpri.org/index.html

Texas Institute for Measurement, Evaluation, and Statistics. 2010. "Technical Report: TPI 2010–2014 Edition." University of Texas and University of Houston. http://www.tpri.org/resources/documents/20102014TechnicalReport.pdf

University of Oregon Center on Teaching and Learning. 2007a. "What are IDEL Measures." Accessed https://dibels.uoregon.edu/training/measures/idelinfo.php.

University of Oregon Center on Teaching and Learning. 2007b. "What Are DIBELS Dynamic Indicators of Basic Early Literacy Skills?" https://dibels.uoregon.edu/training/measures/dibelsinfo.php

Vispoel, Walter P., and James R. Austin. 1995. "Success and Failure in Junior High School: A Critical Incident Approach to Understanding Students' Attributional Beliefs." *American Educational Research Journal* 322: 377–412.

Vygotsky, Lev S. 1978. *Mind in Society: The Development of Higher Psychological Processes.* Cambridge, MA: Harvard University Press.

Wang, K.H., Wang, T.H., Wang, W. L. and Huang, S. C. (2006), Learning styles and formative assessment strategy: enhancing student achievement in Web-based learning. *Journal of Computer Assisted Learning*, 22: 207–217.

Warrington, Stuart D. 2006. "Building Automaticity of Word Recognition for Less Proficient Readers." *Reading Matrix* 61: 52–65. http://www.readingmatrix.com/articles/warrington/article.pdf

Westen, Drew, and Robert Rosenthal. 2003. "Quantifying Construct Validity: Two Simple Measures." *Journal of Personality and Social Psychology* 843: 608–18.

Wiggins, Grant, and Jay McTighe. 2005. *Understanding by Design.* Alexandria, VA: Association for Supervision and Curriculum Development.

Wikipedia. 2013. "What's My Line." Wikipedia, the free encyclopedia. Accessed February 5, 2013. http://en.wikipedia.org/wiki/What's_My_Line%3F

Wininger, Steven R. 2005. "Using Your Tests to Teach: Formative Summative Assessment." *Teaching Psychology* 322: 164–66.

Wirth, Karl R., and Dexter Perkins. 2008. "Learning to Learn." http://www.macalester.edu/academics/geology/wirth/learning.pdf

Wood, David, Jerome S. Bruner, and Gail Ross. 1976. "The Role of Tutoring in Problem Solving." *Journal of Child Psychology and Psychiatry* 172: 89–100.

Yarbrough, Arthur. 2011. "Writing an Effective Writing Prompt." *The Writing Hood Blog*, March 11, 2011. http://writinghood.com/writing/writing-an-effective-writing-prompt/

Zeilik, Michael. "Classroom Assessment Techniques: Concept Mapping." *Field-Tested Learning Assessment Guide for Science, Math, Engineering, and Technology Instructors.* Madison: University of Wisconsin–Madison. Accessed January 15, 2012. http://www.flaguide.org/cat/conmap/conmap7.php

# Index